Fear & Longing

GEMMA OSBORNE
AND
LESLEYANN MORGAN

REDSTONE BOOKS

Copyright © Gemma Osborne and Lesleyann Morgan 2008

First published in 2008 by Serendipity Publishers, Darlington, UK
2nd Edition published in 2008 by Redstone Books, Murton, UK

ISBN 978-0-95608-980-9

Printed and bound by CPI Antony Rowe, Eastbourne

FEAR & LONGING

B

On-lir

ACKNOWLEDGEMENTS

The following people helped us in all sorts of ways. Some were just personally supportive; others were interviewed by us, gave us useful material or helped with the alternative education strategy in one way or another. Different people read our drafts and made us tea - they all contributed to the success we achieved.

Lynda & Geoff, Steph, Aunty Sandra, Granddad, Karen, Andrew, Dennis, Lawrence, Gladys, Terry, John, Julie, Rachael, Ian, Nigel, Jodie, Joe, Alison, Sandy, Gill, Helen and the villagers of Murton.
Sincere thanks to Martin of CPI for your support with this project.

I would like to dedicate this book to my sister, Steph, You were always there for me, a constant support throughout all my difficulties and my best friend who never gave up on me.

Gemma Osborne

This book is a tribute to Gemma, I learned a lot from you kid! I would also like to dedicate it to my husband who never stinted in his support for what I was trying to do even when it seemed to be taking all of my time, his love kept me going.

Lesleyann Morgan

CONTENTS

FOREWORD

The foreword to this book has been written from two main perspectives that represent my work as both a teacher educator and also a therapist. The views are naturally underpinned by my experience of being a mother to three children who for a variety of reasons have been a challenge to the school system.

This is a wonderful and important book that will be of real interest to a wide range of readers. Children and adolescents, educators, parents, therapists and social workers who work with learners and families excluded from mainstream education will gain insight from what is written here. It is as story about 'magic', 'hope' and a love that is unconditional and empowering. It is written with a passion and a sensitivity that gives the reader access to the many challenging processes that both writers are engaged in.

Presented as a parallel dialogue, the layout allows you to read Lesleyann's and Gemma's text one at a time (as I did on the first reading) or together in a way that demonstrates the closeness, intimacy, and yet surprising separateness of the writing.

I am not sure what I love most about the book. Lesleyann provides a reflective and theoretical analysis of the journey while Gemma's writing gives descriptive and yet equally reflective and revealing insights. Read separately they are captivating but together they are very powerful and deeply engaging with each text feeding off the other. There are stories here within stories and shared pivotal moments can be found when real movement takes place that I feel apply equally to both writers.

In a world where we demand instant gratification and results, conformity and individualism we are reminded in this book that there is an alternative and equally effective road to travel, that real relationships take time to build and that achievement comes slowly when it is allowed to emerge from learning processes.

Lesleyann's Story
Lesleyann's use of educational theory to explain the process is very valuable to the reader and gives validity and weight to Gemma's experience and a voice through which she can be heard. She helps Gemma to understand that vocabulary is the key to insight and may also be one of the blockages to Gemma's growth. This is confirmed later in the text when Gemma finds a sense of connection with other writers through reading their poetry

There are strong challenges made to the model of education we have in the compulsory sector and an alternative approach is introduced based on the process of learning rather than the content of the curriculum, which both deepens and broadens the learning. Gemma is supported to become both a qualitative researcher and the researched. There is an important message for educationalists here in that learners who are excluded or exclude themselves from school have not stopped wanting to learn but have lost the capacity to learn in a school environment: school can actually hurt. Throughout the learning activities there is a focus on feedback to Gemma that confirms her success in small stages and raises aspirations.

Lesleyann can best be described as both a teacher and a therapeutic friend to Gemma and it is the strength of this relationship that facilitates her eventual autonomy. At the same time Lesleyann is also a researcher and while Gemma looks down and in to her own processes Lesleyann very effectively looks out at the family and professionals involved. The data collected and used within the text illustrates the gradual enlightenment and self questioning that occurs as individuals challenge their own understanding of appropriate strategies to use with excluded learners. Uncomfortable truths concerning frustration, helplessness and aggression emerge as our natural responses to feeling stuck and hopeless, when even the most gentle of forces from professionals only add to the problems being faced. What is clear is that the 'answer', must lie within the family and be accessed sensitively by professionals who empower rather than remove responsibility.

Gemma's Story

There are some very important insights to be gained from reading Gemma's story. There is a clear vision of her own needs and also her relationship with Leseyann which she describes as having a *'useful distance'* and acknowledges the space this therefore allows her to grow into. She recognises the skills Lesleyann brings to the relationship *'I talked and talked about it; she must have got really bored but she just listened like she always did'* It is often distressing to read the level of physical and mental abuse Gemma has experienced at the hands of bullies. Memories of school, the overwhelming experience of it, the insecurity and fragile nature of the new learner are clearly explained as Gemma tracks the process of losing trust in others. She remembers the restricted curriculum that set boundaries to her imagination and the growing sense of 'falseness' in her relationships. Gemma clearly identifies the qualities of a good teacher, and the subtle behaviours they demonstrate that enable weaker learners to become successful in the classroom. Feeling trapped within the school system by her own fear Gemma sees that there is no alternative to school and so excludes herself. She recognises however that exclusion whether self imposed or not creates an isolation and separateness that is impossible to bridge. There is no going back and Gemma eventually is placed in a position of invisibility from which there feels like no escape.

Gemma's vivid and colourful storytelling provides us with a real insight into how she has seen and faced her own demons, reduced them to size and sorted them out, by the time she has successfully entered college and the world of work she no longer needs them to stay big so that she is able to stay small.

Some notes as a therapist
The parallel dialogue is an excellent away to enable the reader to engage with Lesleann and Gemma's parallel process. The text reveals the use of Humanistic theory where unconditional positive regard, advanced empathy and congruence are both offered to and eventually reciprocated by Gemma. Gemma has a clear awareness of her own vulnerability within the therapeutic relationship as Lesleyann becomes someone who has shared her innermost fears and anxieties. The shared creative and practical activities introduced enable both parties to achieve a high level of congruence and immediacy allowing Gemma to experience the real world in the safe presence of Leslyann rather than being isolated in the world she has created for herself.

Various creative activities were used including fantasy stories and metaphor as a vehicle to allow Gemma to 'tell her story'. There is an opportunity here to transfer inner feelings onto characters external to you and in doing this step back and take control of the characters you are working with. In this context Gemma was able to see the vulnerability within 'Raef' and therefore destroy and cut it down to size. What was wonderful to recognise was that as 'Raef' diminished in both size and power Gemma grew.

The value of 'transitional objects' in working with Gemma especially when linked back to the idea of 'talismans' and the relief that can be brought in simply holding onto a transitional object you have created is highlighted. Additionally the value of structure (agenda) is also introduced as an additional safety net so that Gemma has order she can trust instead of the chaos she is in. Once in place this safety net allows Gemma to trust the process she is engaging in and move onto more creative processes. I believe this structure also allowed Gemma to disintegrate *'fall apart'* at times as she knew she did not have as far to 'fall' as in the past. Structure offered in this way by Lesleyann is containment not confinement and gives an appropriate use of space within the relationship allowing a potential for growth.

This shared experience was clearly therapeutic giving Gemma eventual independence and personal autonomy coupled with the inner resources to continue to maintain this way of being.

I hope that a great many readers enjoy reading this book and take as much from it as I have done.

Alison Barton MBACP

'Can't breath, can't breath…..slow down, slow down, can't stop my hands flapping…this is silly, this is silly…I can't do it….just want to sit here…slow down….slow down…it's ok, it's ok…can't get out of the car…I can't do it…I'm hot…I'm hot…feel sick….it's ok…it's going.' A panic attack, a panic attack in the car outside a college centre, the girl sitting next to me has suddenly become unrecognisable as the child who was eating lunch with me just half an hour ago, where did that confident girl go?

INTRODUCTION

This book is not about panic attacks or phobia, it is not really about being afraid or bullying; it is about longing; longing to be normal and the fear that you never will be again, it is about the legacy of being bullied. It is also about changing that situation.

When you are bullied the first thing that you lose is your confidence, then you lose your dignity, your identity and finally your trust. Trying to regain these is what this book is about; and although you lose your confidence first it is really the last thing that you get back. When it does return it signals the beginning of the end of fear and the realisation of that longed-for normality. Gemma and I have written collaboratively about the experience of re-creating a girl who had been made afraid of her life, how she got back her trust, identity, dignity and confidence. When Gemma began this project she was just fourteen but she hadn't attended school regularly for years. She has written this book for all the other children out there who are struggling to understand what has happened to them.

Hi I'm Gemma:

This book is about me; the me that I was and the me that I am now. What I am really pleased about apart from the success I have had in getting my life back on the tracks is that I have been involved in a piece of research that I hope will help other children. This was not the sort of research that pokes around and looks at other people from the outside, I was doing the poking and looking. I was working out the right questions and asking them myself; I was analysing what was going on inside my head and best of all - I was doing something about it and I have really changed! Being bullied can change your life, but it doesn't need to shut it down completely, that is only one of the things that I have learned. Most importantly I have learned how to understand the way that other people make meaning out of what they do and say, and that your interpretation isn't always the right one.

There are people who seem to have power over you, but that's just how they are, that power doesn't last, and often they have forgotten what they did long before you do - that was my problem, I let it last too long inside my head when it had long ago disappeared from theirs. I stopped going to school for a really long time, all the exam years in fact, but I am now about to begin the dream career that I had in my head before all this happened to me. For quite a long time I thought that I had lost my chance to go to college and be a normal person, but I discovered that I did not have to let all that go I just had to have some guidance to approach it in a different way, re-discover my vision and find a way to make it happen. It was harder work than just attending school but it worked and I hope that by telling you my story I can help you to change yours.

My 'side of the story' is always on the right hand side of the page and the writing always looks like this.

Hello I'm Lesleyann:

This is the story of two people, a girl of fourteen and a retired educationalist who happened to arrive in the same remote village just a month apart, our meeting was a most fortunate happenstance. In this book we tell our stories separately as well as together, they are the stories of a developing friendship, of triumph over fear and an unusual approach to understanding and addressing school phobia that might help another child, their parents, their teachers and their therapists.

The book has been specially devised to be different, each person tells their side of the story on their side of the page, you can read each side separately or you can read the sides in parallel. My side of the page includes the comments of other people such as parents, teachers, psychologists, other writers and theorists, it also contains ideas that I wrote in my journal at the time and notes that were written to me and by me in emails. Some of my side contains whole conversations that I had with a variety of people, I have used their actual words rather than an interpretation of them. Gemma's side of the page is a mixture of critical incident memories, descriptions of her life and metaphor used to explain difficult ideas. Some of the reflections were written at the time in a diary or in notes, some she has reflected on again more recently drawing more and more meaning out of them for her self. This re-reflection provided new learning for her and made her look again at some of the materials we collected over the years. Each section of the book looks at a different factor of the whole issue. All of these elements are also part of our initial analysis of the problem and this is shown in a diagram on page xvii.

One of the most difficult things that teachers and therapists ask of children in distress is to 'tell me how you feel.' Most young people do not have a sufficiently sophisticated vocabulary with which to do this in any depth and so rather than appear to be saying something 'silly', they 'shut down.' This produces the most frustrating situation for parents, teachers and therapists, a distressed child who will not speak to you! When Gemma and I met this was our starting point.

Much of the research into bullying and school phobia is undertaken by psychologists or educationalists who ask questions of young people but who essentially remain outside of the problem looking in, using their own expertise to interpret and try to understand what is going on; but they are nothing like the young people in front of them. Very often these adults will not have had first hand experience of a bullying situation particularly one that prevented their attending school - the fact of their qualification suggests that they completed their education in a normal pattern. Their schooling will have been a fairly uneventful educational experience that needed little explanation at the time; I was like this myself. The research that produced this book was different in that it was a collaborative enterprise, the child at the centre of it was also part of the research team, she was looking *into* as well as *out from* her experiences and this meant that she had to learn the language of research methodology as well as that of introspection and self-reflection. She had to do this in order to properly explain things to me. Whilst this was a challenge to my teaching it also assumed some research significance since it provided her with a more sophisticated vocabulary that enabled her to explain to herself and explore with others, the feelings that she experienced. As her vocabulary increased so the shut down periods decreased, delving into the depth of an experience became an interesting thing to do rather than a perceived threat. My co-researcher was examining herself; and at the same time she was effectively curing herself. The power of appropriate vocabulary is one of the important discoveries of this research. Gemma began to love using the words that she discovered to explain her feelings.

While I was researching the topic of school phobia I also had to provide a legitimate and interesting learning experience to replace Gemma's lost schooling. We have tried to include as much as we can about this 'study skills' programme because many of the activities are unusual and the way that we combined them may be a useful model for those working with other children in similar situations. As Gemma developed her understanding of the way that meanings are constructed she learned to be more philosophical about how people's acts and statements had affected her, and she could begin to analyse and then dismiss her 'demons' in order to take more control of her life. Of course how this happened is part of the research, and it was quite a 'messy' (post-modern) process but all the more fun for that! *'I feel really pleased with myself that I did that, I'm not used to feeling happy, it's almost scary!'*

Attending school regularly from the age of four to the age of sixteen or seventeen is the most straightforward way to prepare for a future career but it is not the only way to do it, as we discovered!

We are truly grateful to all the people who gave their time to help us; who tried to understand and support what we were doing and who talked to us about their work and their own experiences. We have endeavoured to represent all of this soul searching in the different sections of this book. Apart from Gemma's immediate family all names have been changed, or removed in the case of the professionals interviewed. Where a job description or role was important to an understanding of the text this has been given but in the most part the value of the ideas that crop up in conversations and that are set out here is implied and left open to the readers interpretation as it suits their situation.

*'I thought bullying was only when it was something physical, like someone hitting you....that did happen, I did get pushed in the road, but that wasn't the worst, the worst bit was when they ignored me like I didn't exist...people who had been my friends started a whispering thing....I felt so completely alone..... couldn't face school then...they were right, I was a nothing! That was my **fear**, but also there was a **longing** to belong again that I just couldn't confront or resolve.'*

'When I looked at those girls on my course I realised that I would have been girly like that if this hadn't happened to me, I am not sure if I felt a loss or an achievement when I looked at them. I am a different person now, in some ways much more mature, in others still a child with no experience of being a 'normal' teenager - I had that ground to make up when I got to college.'

'One of the most important things in the early days of us working together was that you asked the <u>right</u> questions you listened to me and you weren't at all judgmental!'

'Once I learned the language of reflection I got really interested in describing my feelings, writing everything down and getting deeply inside the issues, a lot of my early journal material here is quite basic, but as I got better at probing myself and learned more interesting words that were really descriptive of my feelings the writing got so much better. I hope that you can see this in the final chapter, where I reflected on my reflections and still discovered new learning there.'

We are not assuming that teachers or other professionals will have the time to work with students in the way that we worked, nor will they be able to give this much time to supporting the many students in their care. The amount of time I was able to give to Gemma was unusually high but that allowed us to surface and explore a great many issues that will be of interest to parents and professionals. Our working strategies offer an insight into aspects of this problem that might not be revealed in the normally short times that are available to work with students and it is these factors that we hope may prove a useful resource or a comfort whichever you need at the time. The text is one to dip into, a patchwork composed of conversations, theories, ideas and reflections that we are sure will find resonance with our readers.

'When I was fourteen my life as a normal teenager had come to a stop really, I couldn't be bothered to get up and get dressed so I was spending an awful lot of time in my rabbit pyjamas!'

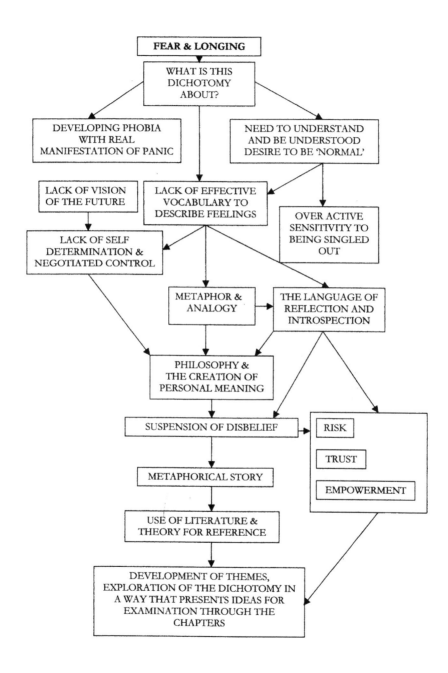

"The important things in life always happen by accident. At fifteen she didn't know much, in fact, with each passing year she was a lot less clear about most things. But this much she did know. You could worry yourself sick trying to be a better person [...]... And then out of the black beyond, like a hawk on a rat, some nameless catastrophe would swoop into your life and turn everything upside down and inside out forever.'

(from the *Smoke Jumper* - Nicholas Evans 2002:15)

CHAPTER ONE

Serendipity

A story comprises events, actions and outcomes, but it is only the interpretation of these factors by the characters that creates the story. In fact the characters in a story act within the events in a parallel way, their simultaneous interpretations are founded on individual prior experiences and knowledge and this is what influences and causes the outcomes. Activity theory (Follett, 1924) suggests that in any situation the dynamic created by inter-relation of environment, stimulus and action causes a response that modifies all these components, creating the next situation and the next response.

This story is no different.

The girl sitting next to me in the car is so withdrawn into herself that I am reminded of Spencer's (1996:89) accurate description of a young person.... 'sat down in a loosejointed, dissociated, teenage way that often said, *Read my mind.*'

I tried to but I couldn't. All I was doing was a neighbourly thing of taking her to the station to catch a train to the local city for her weekly attendance at a pupil referral centre. I knew of her school attendance problems but

Fear & Longing

Around Easter of my first Secondary school year I had some time off school. I don't think I had anything bad, I was just 'off colour'. I think that I was consciously not really enjoying school by then, if I had been then probably I would have gone in, but I didn't. I stayed at home. I was away for about a week; when I went back everything had changed.

It was so much safer at home, so much more protected from the complications of school, of friendship groups, of the need to grow up. What really got to me was that my friends were starting to get boyfriends and all they could do was talk about boys, look at boys and get stupid and giggly. That made me feel pressured about why I didn't want one (a boyfriend). There was so much pressure to 'fit in' and do the normal thing, go out with a boy for a week or two and drop him, take up with someone else, tell all your friends about what had happened and what you did. This level of pressure to be like everyone else just got to me. It wasn't a major pressure but I got annoyed with it all and my friends started to act really girly. Sex oriented 'girly' is very different to the ordinary girly stuff that we had indulged in, magazines and clothes, bitchiness. This was more about 'show' to impress boys; th' 'opped being natural. I still liked t   '' had become so differen
very difficult to relc
used to listen to m
now they had n
embarrassed by
that they consic

1

only in a relatively shallow way from talking to her mother, and as a retired teacher helping these parents to understand the role of a clinical psychologist when the appointment was offered to them. I really don't know this girl at all.

'once they were in secondary school...she was quite excited about starting...they feel grown up, don't they...she went off with her friend the first morning, quite positively...I can still picture them going off. The first few weeks everything was pretty ok, I think. She had a few days off sick, but then these things happen, don't they...?'

The train is on strike, we have turned around to drive back home. I want to know this girl a bit more; she is suddenly so relaxed to be going home and I want to know why. I know that she likes the independence of travelling to the city, she likes the referral centre, and the staff there and this weekly visit is giving her back some motivation for life...but clearly not enough.

We talk more than we have before and I realise that although she might be described as a school refuser, she is not refusing education. She just does not want to be taught in a school, where because of the actions of others and her own interpretation [of] them she feels unsafe and [insecu]re. She is an intelligent girl [at]tentive and interested in [idea]s and concepts. I am

I'm sitting here in my kitchen with this woman, who up to now, I have not had much to do with. Before, she was just a neighbour who I know used to be a teacher but now she is here with me and wants to know what happened at school. I don't know why but I feel ok about this. Maybe because if it was Mum or Dad, they would end up getting upset. They are always upset at the moment. We all are. I begin to explain briefly about my past. I feel like I have said this so many times to so many 'experts' who try to help me but this time I feel more at ease, maybe because I am tired. I feel so drained and dead at the moment. She seems nice and unlike the others, she isn't trying to force me into horrible situations. For some reason she just seems interested in what happened and I want to tell her but it is so hard to explain. There is a useful distance about her, she isn't part of any of this. I feel cold and I mumble out a few things without really looking at her. I don't feel embarrassed, just pathetic ... She seems to ask the right questions and I am not being judged. I don't feel any need to either impress or annoy her, I just know that she won't be affected by anything I tell her; that's weird but also very comforting. We have started work on the research!

Everyone at school wanted to grow up, wanted to do grown up scary things. I didn't want to grow up, I have a younger sister and we always do everything together, and because my childhood was so happy and safe I didn't want to leave it behind. So in this way I got left behind everyone else; they thought that fun was going out and I thought that fun was having my friends around to my house and going across the fields and just mucking around—making the most of our youth, I suppose. I didn't want to lose my innocent view of the world. I guess my schoolfriends wouldn't have understood that. Matt probably an educational philosopher: could I teach her philosophy and enable her to make more rational sense of what she is experiencing?

Psychologists who deal with behavioural issues such as bullying, truancy and disaffection are on the outside of the problem looking in; they require the 'client' to give a verbal description of their 'feelings'. The vocabulary for this level of deep personal reflection is sophisticated and certainly not the norm for young people. Some of it is crucial to being able to describe such feelings and they just don't have it.

'What you just said, that is very important and it's one of the many issues that has probably passed me by over the years as an educational psychologist. The parallel in academic terms would be the increasing emphasis on pupils learning the vocabulary of the subject, in education we recognise that they can't be an effective mathematician even at key stage 1 unless they have that vocabulary, and similarly we teach 'key words' to children in literacy. Good work in emotional literacy at key stage 3 & 4 in the last few years has been devoted to teaching the vocabulary around these concepts, the upskilling of the pupil if you like, so that they can talk rationally with understanding about these issues. I recognise now that this idea has passed me by in relation to students like Gemma—when we ask those well intentioned questions—'how are

understood it but he never really said so, I think he liked the fact that I was a bit non-conformist in a non-threatening way. Hey! This is me reflecting and I probably wouldn't have got close to this truth at the time.

'I can't find the right words to describe how I feel, and by the time I have the person has got fed up and made a decision anyway—I don't mind really.'

When I was off school for whatever reason I had 'manufactured' I watched TV—anything that was on, sometimes the old films, but anything that would allow me to escape from the real world for whole hours at a time. Mum was assuming I was 'off colour' and so cleaned around me and got on with her normal housework. She didn't work during the day so she was there for me really—was that one of the reasons I could do this? At the beginning I would have two or three days off and eventually I would have to go back. A month or two might go by, or sometimes only a week or two before I would be feeling that it was too much for me and I had to have a space of time away from it again. My Dad didn't really know much about this situation that was being created as he was working full time and often had left before I would have been going to school and would arrive back after the time when I might normally have returned. Although I supposed Mum talked about it with him, I certainly didn't.

If I'm honest all I ever wanted was to be Dad's princess. I know that I spoiled that myself, but I didn't know that at the time. Why couldn't he make it better for me, I wanted my friends back as we had been before things changed. Change like this can't be reversed. I've learned that.

I think the trouble was that I was very

you feeling?' we've all experienced that 'shut down', the 'I don't know', the blankness and we've just put it down to their emotional turmoil, and we were wrong—if they don't know the words how can they talk about it?'

Philosophy on the other hand requires people to look within themselves at how they create the meanings that they do and how this 'sensemaking' might be interpreted by others. Developing a philosophical understanding of events and actions can go on inside your head; you don't have to expose it to the scrutiny of others unless you choose to do so in conversation. Thus whilst psychological activities may help the psychologist relate to how you react to people and situations if you can explain it well enough to him, he will not really understand how you think, or what that thinking has made you feel like. Developing an understanding of philosophy including emotional and empathic awareness and intelligence, together with a vocabulary for explaining it might enable you as a person to change your own thinking in an emancipatory and strategic way.

'When people kept asking me how I felt, I didn't have the words to explain it, so I just shut down, and in shutting down to others I was just going over and over in my head how to explain what I was feeling, even to myself.'

Gemma is an intelligent girl; if forgiving, I was the perfect victim. I didn't bear grudges, didn't fight back, I just let it happen and if I did tell anyone then I was just told to 'stay away from them then.' This isn't really possible, kids can always find other kids wherever they hide. Darren was a very clever boy, he always scored merits so it was probably difficult for teachers to believe bad things of him. I am sure that some teachers knew he could be horrible, but school is about performing and doing the work and he could certainly do that when required. He was infuriating and I really hated him because he was in control so much.

When I was behind with my school work, I did these extra classes and I was walking home from one of these when I saw Darren coming in the opposite direction on his bike. 'Hello ugly girl,' he said (his pet name for me!). He tried to suggest that I had been in detention; not wanting more teasing I did not admit to the extra classes. He rode off and I thought that was it. Suddenly I heard the bike coming up from behind, I was waiting for his voice, and the bike came closer and closer then suddenly I felt his front wheel go into my legs and I was pushed into the road. A car was coming round the corner, luckily not close enough to hit me and I managed to get out of the way. Darren was laughing—I called him something and he just rode away. I went home and told my Dad; he got really angry and threatened to give Darren a piece of his mind, but he never did in the end. I don't think that Darren told anyone about what had happened or what he had done, In my memory this event did not accelerate any of the name calling or shunning that was going on.

In my mind things were going from bad to worse; sustaining attendance was getting harder and harder and it was easier and easier to be 'ill'. I found

I am going to help her in the way that I am suggesting here it must be through a method that has innovative appeal. On that journey from the station I resolved to formulate a research project in which she could become a co-researcher and author. *'When I arrived home, I worked all afternoon on a project proposal which I delivered to Gemma's Mum. I am not sure how this family will react to my proposal, I can only wait and see.'*

Gemma's parents are relieved that someone is suggesting that there may be a way out of this stalemate situation. The pressure to 'get her back to school' is telling on them. Gemma has become entrenched in her aversion tactics to the extent that she will not get out of bed if there is any sort of suggestion that she might try attending school or meet with a professional who may have this agenda. She sets her mouth; her eyes look into a middle distance and she shuts down as completely as it is possible for a human being to do. I am reminded of pictures of prisoners who go inside themselves to a world less traumatic than the one they are in. I need to offer her a non-threatening way to probe her feelings. I will endeavour to teach her how to be a qualitative researcher; this will involve reflection and analysis. I hope that the act of researching interpretively will become therapeutic, but this can only be done at her own pace; she has to find her own voice and style, her own way of coming to an

myself wanting to be ill, really ill, so that I had a real reason to be away for a very long time and maybe never go back. I had got to the point where I stopped pretending to be ill and just said I don't want to go.' My natural stubbornness kicked in and I refused to be forced, fear hit me each time that I awoke in the morning and I felt scared in a way that I couldn't explain. The horrible alarm clock that sounded like a fire drill forced me out of sleep in a traumatic way and things could only get worse from that moment on. When I knew it was daytime I would pull the covers over my head hoping it would go away. I would try to force myself back to sleep and Mum would come in. I don't think that she had any idea what she could do about it; I certainly didn't.

The local Secondary school here in this new place is old and housed in grounds in the town. My previous school had over 1,500 pupils, this one has no more than 750, it's bound to be ok here, isn't it?

On the first day of our new lives in the North my sister and I waited in the village for the school bus. She was going to the primary school, I was off to the secondary school. I was nervous, but it was a normal nervous not an insane nervous. When I arrived at the school I was worried about where to go but the Headmaster had arranged for two older girls to meet me off the bus. I was shown where my class was and met two other girls who I soon became friends with. It was weird being in a school with these 'northerners' after living with the familiar Essex accent but I liked them. The problem was me. I had become so wary and reserved, everyone was so friendly and chatty towards me, I must have seemed snobby and a bit distracted.

Some girls seemed a bit bitchy towards me and I think I was a bit scared that the past was going to happen all over understanding of her self-imposed prison.

Gemma will become both the researcher and the 'researched'. This case study methodology will give her a reason to find out how to be introspective in a strategic way. If I can use the research methods as teaching tools, then perhaps we can both learn from this task in different and innovative ways. Gemma will be trying to focus on what is going on inside her head and body in order to explain it to me; this will be the physical manifestations of her 'feelings' - what is a panic attack, what does it actually feel like? It is far less threatening to ask a child to describe exactly how it feels to be sick than to ask. 'How does it *feel* to be bullied.' Particularly if the bullying is not physical. That type of question is far down the line and requires a new emotionally descriptive vocabulary which has yet to be taught. The relationship between feeling sick and anticipating being bullied is a subtle one that will need to be understood by this girl if she is to begin to make sense of what is happening to her. I will be learning how to respond effectively to the possibly strange inner workings of a teenage girl's mind; respond in a way that supports, encourages and engages her and enables her to take more control of the way her life is going. I sense that she feels 'out of control' of her own emotions, wants to be rid of them on the one hand but is sheltering inside them, *'drawing the covers*

again. It feels stupid when I think about it now but everything was different and I didn't have my old friends, these people already had friends and I was just the new girl. I thought that in the end the same stuff would happen again and I would end up alone. For no real reason other than letting non-existent things get on top of me I began to have time off again.

After my conversation with the woman who drives me to the station she thought of an idea. Mum hands over a piece of paper explaining a project. I do read it carefully and I feel a bit surprised, I would never have thought that this problem of mine could be useful. It will give me something to do, I suppose, and maybe some good will come out of it for other children.

Writing things down helped me a lot. There are memories and incidents that I think I should make a note of because they had an influence on me. If I write them down then I can piece things together and they show me why I felt and behaved oddly back then. I kept all these notes and now years after starting scribbling my feelings down, I can look at it in a more rational way and see them for what they are. This is something I couldn't do properly 3 or 4 years ago because I was still going through it and I didn't have the language. Once things were on paper, they were more out of my system. Before I had just gone over things again and again which made everything worse. I began to think *too* much and it wasn't good for me to do that. These thoughts and feelings were mainly bitter and they depressed me. I felt like a mad woman. When I started writing things down they were written in harsh scribbles and they came across quite dark and twisted. I wrote some of this stuff to Lesleyann because I wanted my feelings to be known to someone other than me, someone who wouldn't *over her head'* on the other hand.

Learning to write a journal will be one of the hardest things that this girl has done, and at first I must ensure that she knows that she is writing it for herself. At this stage I will not be able to read it, so will not know if she is doing it in an effective way. Hopefully as she surfaces some of the difficult ideas in her writing she will bring them to our discussions. I want to use the journal eventually to tell her story; her journal will provide the critical incident way of writing which will be easier for her than any idea of chronology. When you remember things it is disjointed, ideas snap into your mind, or memories are jogged by other happenings: this, I hope, is eventually the way we will write.

The project will be called 'Fear and Longing', a title that we both feel comfortable with because it is insightful of the dichotomy of feelings that are related to issues of bullying, school refusal and phobia. This research project will be a qualitative examination of what is involved in being a school phobic, and importantly we need to discover how to help such a student emerge from the results of this trauma to a life beyond. Gemma has to cross the threshold so that she can provide evidence that it is possible.

judge me by them. I couldn't show my family because they would not have liked what they saw and it would have made things worse and worse.

I'm not sure if I can be very helpful but why not? The idea of it makes me feel important for the first time in a while. I think I am going to be a sort of apprentice and that does sound interesting. *'We have decided to call the project Fear and Longing: those two words sum up everything really.'*

I can give it a go. I don't have to do this, she made that very clear, so it's my turn to have a choice in something. She wants me to control how this research goes, she says that I am the one who really knows how it will work because I am inside the problem so I am the only one who can really explain it. She can help me to learn how to do it, but she is outside. I have to write a sort of diary, a journal of my thoughts—whatever they are, writing, she says, will help me. I don't have to show her but I can if I want to. And we will have sort of lessons about research.

This is such a cool idea— we go off to the library to look for books and she asks me to find a book on the education book shelf that seems to be about alternative education. I have NO IDEA what I am looking for, but I find a book that is called 'Learning Beyond the Classroom'; it seems about right. It looks very academic, not my sort of book, and I am suddenly very unsure that I know what we are doing, but she looks at it and is REALLY impressed with my find—maybe I can do this work after all. We order the book to come to our library and we have started on our project. Our project, not her project. I've got a job!

CHAPTER TWO

Meaning & Metaphor

Using analogy or metaphor allows a deconstruction of principal ideas, and as Claxton (1990:115) indicates, it *'is like taking an established minitheory and stripping it of most of its content and floating it into a new area, the domain of the problem.'* This, he suggests, provides a vantage point from which the puzzle may begin to make sense.

People make sense of situations through an interpretation of circumstances, and this is based on their prior knowledge and experience, and their viewpoint which may be influenced by age, status, expectations, predictions and how they want to present themselves and their understandings to others. This potential positioning of an 'observer' as being something that is not particularly stable is not often discussed as a concept; but it is in fact vital to understanding how others may be drawing their conclusions about *your* actions.

As Gemma learns more about the use of metaphor and analogy she has a way of exploring and presenting her problems that may be less embarrassing for her—a narrative 'voice' she has never had before in trying to describe her beliefs and feelings.

During our discussions at the

Hold on to a Dream

Long ago in Algeza, a small dusty town at an oasis in the desert where things were never quite what they seemed, there was an old but pretty farm building. Inside lived a husband—Oz, his wife Jeena, and their two daughters, Jas and Bindi. The two sisters spent a lot of time together and caused mischief when they were younger. At this point of their lives Jas was beginning to come out of childhood. She loved to make things and to sew with scraps of fabric that she found outside the dressmaker's house. Bindi was still quite young—the baby of the family. She was always on the go and enjoyed getting messy. She did not have to worry about her future just yet. Jas thought about what she would like to do. She had always wanted to sell her own crafts on her very own stall at the most beautiful end of the market. The only problem was that she was too afraid to do it. Although all the people in her life, including the Wise Woman of the East, believed in her, Jas just couldn't believe in herself. Jas wasn't always like this but for some reason she had changed and become withdrawn over the past few years.

On a hot and very dry afternoon, Jas was walking through Algeza along with her faithful friend Tops the dog. She found herself in the market place. It was buzzy with different sounds and vibrant colours. On the West Side was the farmers' market, which sold all sorts of food and working tools. Her house was at the West End too. But through all this she could always get a glimpse of the East End through her bedroom window.

Whenever she went to market, Jas would always end up at the eastern start of our work programme, it became increasingly clear that whilst Gemma was actively trying to surface some of the difficult issues, she was still struggling with effective vocabulary with which to do it. I have found in my own work that when faced with a difficult to understand situation, working out an acceptable and effective metaphor or analogy allows you to explore it differently and because you need to link all the issues to viable similes, this pushes at the boundaries of the analogy and it is that task that gives you insight into what the whole problem or dilemma might be about.

First of all we talked a great deal about the background to some common fairy stories and nursery rhymes. Some of this information was unknown to her and surprised her a great deal. Then I used some short passages where normal ideas were challenged by the way that they were used; good examples of this can be found in *Winnie the Pooh*. In my journal I wrote:

'Today I used a passage from Pooh *and The Philosophers (Tyerman Williams, 1997) in which Pooh sees Rabbit and says, 'Is that you, Rabbit?' Rabbit replies, 'Let's pretend it isn't and see what happens!' We discussed this idea of suspension of disbelief for some time. If we convert reality into a present world, not only might we understand it differently but perhaps temporarily we give ourselves control over the outcomes.'*

I constructed a number of tiny stories using metaphor and analogy to show Gemma how this idea

side. It was like magic and was so beautiful because it sold things like party dresses spangled with sequins and saris printed in all sorts of shades including gold and silver. There was jewellery and ornaments with gems and diamonds. There were strange objects that had been found and brought back from distant lands and over the seas. The whole place seemed to glow as you walked through it and at night lanterns were lit everywhere so that it looked like a beacon from a distance. As Jas strolled around she saw her mother and the Wise Woman whispering to each other. They both stood at the end of the market on the border of the desert. Jas noticed her mother looking worried as the Wise Woman took something out of her robes and placed it on the ground next to a crag of rock. Jas walked over to a stall selling jewellery and she admired a very expensive looking necklace. When she looked up, her mother and the Wise Woman were nowhere to be seen. As Jas stood there, she felt as though everyone was looking at her. She started to feel worried and lowered her head. Suddenly a child shouted nearby which startled her. She panicked and started to run. The vendor yelled and then chased after her. Jas then realised that she still had the necklace, but she couldn't think straight as the panicky feeling got worse so on she ran. She could see people's concerned faces blurred around her as she flashed past them with Tops at her side. The vendor eventually gave up when they reached the edge of the market and got tired of running. As he tried to catch his breath and gasped at a stitch searing through him, something made him look down and he noticed a piece of sandstone on the ground. It was the same piece that the Wise Woman had placed there. He picked it up and hurled it in the direction of Jas's figure in the distance.

Jas stopped. She was in such a state that she did not realise that she was out in the open desert. Hardly anyone went out this far because they got lost, as there were might work. I took real incidents from my own life and produced them as stories; some changed me into a third person looking at the situation so having a different standpoint as a viewer rather than a participant. Others turned people into animals, or situations into fantasy. As Gemma did not know the reality of the events, she had to use her understanding of the story to try to get at the truth of the situation. Aristotle states (in *Polanyi,* 1975, 1977:75) *'a good metaphor implies an intuitive grasp of the similarity in dissimilars.'* Often in her deductions about my stories Gemma was uncomfortably accurate:

'So because your Mum is dead and you can't tell her this now, writing this story is a way of making amends for something you did as a child, almost like you have told her you are sorry. Did you feel better when you had written this....is it something you have been worrying about for a long time?' My answer to all of these questions was 'Yes'.

The result of this strategy to enable her to use another way into her locked up emotions and diminished self was her Jas story. It was most definitely *a* turning point but not *the* turning point.

This type of refocusing on events does not allow you to turn back the clock, but perhaps it allows you to take your time in rewinding it. Recovery is a slow process, slower than we think, metaphorically this enables you to halt your inexorable progress through time for a moment or two while you look at things in more detail. One of the common

no landmarks to guide them. In every direction there were just endless sand dunes. It was starting to get dark and the wind was getting stronger. Jas looked at the few stars starting to show in the distance and then suddenly saw a huge wave of sand block them out. It was heading her way. She quickly covered her face and started to run for home but the sandstorm was way too fast and caught up with her. Within seconds it surrounded her and Tops. Jas covered Tops with her robe as something hard hit her on the head and knocked her out. The sandstone which the vendor had thrown had been carried by the wind; as it hit her it split into two and something fell out and landed beside her, just as the Wise Woman had known it would.

Intense heat woke Jas up the next day. Luckily Tops was still there and well protected by her gown but something else was with them and was pressing uncomfortably into Jas's back. She felt around and saw a shiny object lying half-buried beneath her. She picked it up and shook it free of sand. It was a Genie lamp, which looked as though it was made of silver. Jas had heard stories about magic lamps. People wished for things and they came true. Jas would have loved her dreams to come true but she was also too scared for them to be real. She picked up the lamp and headed for home.

Her family were relieved to have her back home safe again and after a few days' rest, a lady called Mrs Monsoon who lived nearby came to visit. Jas's mother called her from the kitchen. When she arrived, Mrs Monsoon asked if Jas would mind her stall for the day, as she had to help the Wise Woman in the making of a wedding dress and was too busy to do it herself. Jas at first refused, it would be just too scary, but after her mother and the lady had pleaded with her to be helpful for just one day, in the end she had no option so to the market she went.

features of our discussions was the rapid progress of time, a day off quickly became a week, a month, a term. Childhood raced towards adulthood, responsibility, a career and independence, there was no stopping it.

'I think that I am probably quite worried about growing up, I don't really want to lose sight of my childhood.'

Unfortunately the innocence of youth is a terminal condition, vulnerable to the machinations of others who unwittingly or deliberately turn normality into chaos. When this chaotic way of life becomes normality *'It's safer to stay unhappy, I know how to deal with that.'* Then it can be very difficult to change a way of thinking, as Bentley (1998:133) so rightly states:

'We also have thinking dispositions: tendencies to think in particular ways. If there are weaknesses in the way we think, and for all of us there are some, we might tend towards fuzzy thinking, hasty thinking, sprawling thinking which wanders back and forth without clarity or apparent purpose, or narrow thinking which fails to recognise things that go against the grain of what we want to believe.'

The first version of Jas, was written quite quickly and was clearly based on an amalgam of traditional children's stories, but it gave her a starting point to turn ideas into substance. The desert storm was the muddle and whirling of her thoughts; there were elements that clearly related to hiding the truth

When she first started, all she could think of was running back to her nice safe house. So many people, so much noise, so many questions. At least Tops was with her, lying in the shade beneath the stall. When she felt really anxious Jas glanced down and Tops looked up wagging his tail and seeming to smile back at her. At first she was nervous just serving people, and taking their money, then it was only if they asked her a question but as she started to relax a bit she found herself making conversation, encouraging them to buy things. It was almost enjoyable, almost just what she wanted.

At mid-day, Jas suddenly looked across and saw her sister's face gazing at her over the stall. Her chocolate covered lips spread into a cheeky grin. Jas's father was talking to the vendor a few stalls down. 'I'm sorry about my daughter...I can pay you. How much chocolate did she take?' He then walked over to them and glared at Bindi, then gave them some good news. 'Mrs Monsoon is going on a trip with the Wise Woman to get some more materials to stock up with; she can't work on the stall tomorrow so she asked if you could take over again. She also said that because she has run out of things to sell, you can put some of your own stuff on it too.' Jas was so excited. It would be as if *she* owned the stall. 'Can I help Jas?' asked Bindi who nearly knocked a whole case of sapphire rings flying on the next stall. 'Err...No!' said their father and he walked back to their house with Bindi stomping behind him, sweets falling from her sticky fingers.

Jas's excitement suddenly switched to doubt. What if it went horribly wrong? What if she couldn't sell her work? What if...? All sorts of problems came to her mind and the next day for some silly unknown reason, she felt afraid and decided to walk away from the situation before she had a chance to ruin it.

She ran and ran across the sand dunes, far out into the desert, but something suddenly made her stop. The wind blew from people, to being lonely, to not being able to succeed in her life and then to finding joy and being encouraged by 'The Wise Woman of the East.'

We left the story as it was for some time and originally it was called 'Kissy Wissy and the Magic Lamp.' She was unhappy with this as it seemed too childish and girly. Gemma as co-researcher became very concerned that our work would have resonance for both girls and boys, so she did not want a title or the content to put off readers; certainly a more neutral name for the 'hero/heroine' became very important and we scanned the papers looking for ethnic names that suited the story but were not particularly gender specific.

Echoes of the story construction remained around us for some time after she had written it, and I regularly received little notes addressed to 'The Wise Woman of the East'. This level of collaboration in writing was a very new concept for Gemma and she began to sense the value in what she was being asked to do.

As her vocabulary developed so she improved the story and it became more and more her own work rather than merely a cannibalised fairy tale. She also began to delve more deeply into the individual ideas within the story, in particular working in a maniacal fashion on ways to describe her 'demon', finding horror pictures in books and magazines that could be 'it'. It was interesting that the demon was not a he or she, so not a person but a situation; perhaps 'it' was the

eerily. She could hear a voice. A cold whisper. It was calling her name but no one was there. Then quite suddenly something pulled her to the ground. She lay there in horror as the sand shifted and rose above her forming a human shape.

Whatever it was spoke to her and said that it's name was *Raef*, said it nastily. *'You will never stop me getting inside your head and preventing you being happy...never...never...remember Jas, I am the 'demon-inside'.* It stood laughing at her, making her feel miserable.

Then to her surprise it sort of smiled...it was hard to tell if it was a smile but it spoke in a gentle, cold and persuasive voice. It moved in closer to her and filled her with a menacing chill. *'It is much safer and better if you just give up,'* it whispered. *'You don't really want to be happy because you know it won't last, at least you can always count on loneliness because there is no-one there to let you down...it is too much of a risk to try to be happy...in the end it gets taken away... you know that's right, don't you?'*

There was something in those words that felt so true to Jas and with them in her head all her hopes and dreams disintegrated. *'Why not come with me?'* said Raef and held out its hand.

From behind her, Jas could hear familiar voices calling her name. It was her family and the Wise Woman of the East. Jas's mother rushed up and quickly grabbed hold of her arm and dragged her back towards Algeza but Jas was trying to fight her off and so struggled all the way back. *'Just let it take me...'* she said.

Jas's family and the Wise Woman of the East were surprised and shocked when Jas's personality changed over the next few days. She was rude and stubborn and did not speak to anyone unless she had to. She wouldn't go out or do anything useful and she just kept disappearing every so often and no one whole issue of being controlled by fear, and right from the beginning the demon was called 'Raef'.

Surfacing some of this murk, from the swampy lowlands of her experiences gave her a non-threatening way to introduce me to some of the characteristics of her past, to what may actually have happened to her that had become subsumed into a phobic reaction to school. Because of working on the character of 'Raef', we explored all the possible definitions of bullying and forms of repressive behaviour and a new picture emerged of the background to this situation in which she felt trapped by circumstances, events and most of all by fear. What also transpired was a quite immature understanding of what constituted bullying behaviour. *'Are you saying that shunning and ignoring can also be called bullying?'* It's called repressive behaviour, putting people down, but yes, it is a form of bullying. *'I thought bullying was only physical, punching and fighting and stuff.'*

When a child is not attending school, then anxieties such as these are nurtured by lack of stimulii usually provided by school work and friends. As these pupils have fewer and fewer distractions in their lives, to interest them or to talk about, they focus inwardly, firstly on the apparent causes of their situation, then more destructively on themselves and their own perceived shortcomings. *'How did I cause this?'* Their vulnerability is enhanced by having no other image of themselves than the one that they have constructed

knew where she got to. All they could find were pieces of paper with the word 'Fear' written all over them in her room. She had left her life behind her and refused help or guidance from anyone who came her way. It was as though she was possessed and even her little sister's jokes seldom made her smile.She sat day in day out, haunted by those words that she had heard, believing them to be completely true. In the end those days turned into years and although she was still afraid of life, Jas began to secretly yearn for it deep inside. But she couldn't have it. It was not allowed. It was much safer to carry on as she was.

One night Jas went out to the desert again. It was somewhere for her to hide. She sat down in the sand and saw the stars in the distance. Jas thought of her family and a future that could be filled with warmth but those thoughts were quickly wiped out by a tide of sand which came towards her and again formed the shape of Raef. Despite its presence, Jas still felt warm and had an image of her sister laughing and playing. Maybe happiness was worth fighting for. All of a sudden Raef did not seem so safe and reliable. Instead of a haven, loneliness felt like a prison and she wanted to get away and so desperately wanted her life back.

Something inside Jas suddenly clicked and all that despair turned to strength. She drew a piece of paper from her pocket with the word 'Fear' written at the top. She stared at it and then got a pen and wrote that same word back to front. Now on the paper beneath the first word it said 'Raef'. *'So that's it!'* she said. *'I'm going backwards instead of forwards with my life!'* Suddenly she remembered the lamp. She took it from her robes and stood with it in her hands in the middle of the swirling sand. She knew what to do.

Jas stared at Raef. She could not really see its face. If this object wasn't real how could it hurt her? How could it control to account for their position. This is in effect a loss of identity.

'I was shocked as well, that this was my daughter; that was suddenly...this behaviour was totally out of character and I just couldn't recognise her any more, there were these determined steel like features. I thought where has this come from?...that scared me.'

'As a clinical psychologist I am aware that when a child is not attending school then anxiety levels are usually sky high, the parents, the teachers, educational welfare and inevitably the young person, so there may be medical or psychological issues to do with anxiety. There is often a query about depression if the young person has become withdrawn, and so those two things are the most common reason for a referral to us.'

Attending school is not the only way to obtain an education; it is the easiest and most direct route to a career but it is invested with a cruciality that is frightening to non-attenders who may be victims of circumstances beyond their control. The panic attacks described in this work may be attributed to this and other fears.

what she did? It did not have the power to decide what she wanted. Suddenly Jas couldn't see what was powerful about this 'creature' at all.

'You're not real,' she said. 'I really don't need this.' And she hurled the lamp towards the column of sand that was forming into Raef. The demon reeled and then leaned forward trying to scare her again...but somehow it just didn't seem at all threatening. Jas smiled and then began to laugh.

Raef screamed in pain and lurched forwards but when it struck it didn't hurt a bit. It really was not real. Jas picked up the lamp (it was silver after all!) and started to walk away, ignoring the yelling of her demon. She never turned back, not until she reached the town. She expected when she looked around that the column of sand would still somehow be there behind her but it had completely disappeared. The desert was still, silent and strangely beautiful. She looked towards the market with its twinkling lamps and she did not feel afraid of working there. Instead she felt happy and safe to wander back through it; it contained her future life and home, the place where she belonged.

Within a month, Jas had sold the lamp on her very own stall, at the most beautiful end of the market, without making a wish...

The wish she had wanted had already come true.

CHAPTER THREE

Phobia:
Intelligence eroded by fear

Ivan Ward (2001:73) has stated:

> *'If all phobias were dynamically or genetically similar in many important ways, calling a symptom a phobia would be useful. In fact, however, the reverse is the case. The only thing all phobias have in common is the defensive use of avoidance. They share nothing else, either dynamically or genetically, which distinguishes them from any other class of symptoms.'*

My mother was one of the strongest women I have ever met, in terms of both her practicality and her personality. In 1948 as a young woman of less than 19 she had followed her soldier husband to the far east, endured the Karen Uprising in Burma with a young baby, packed and repacked numerous homes as they travelled around the world and in the early days brought up two young children alone when my father was away. One tough lady. As a young teenager I would sometimes arrive home from school to find all the doors and windows open and her locked in the bathroom because a bird had flown into the house and she was terrified of it. I would have to search around to find the poor creature if it hadn't already escaped and then tell her when I was sure that it was not anywhere about. She loved birds in the normal course of events but

Suspension of Disbelief

I once had a friend, she let me down. I have always felt small next to her, as she always seemed to be happy and had everything she wanted. Whenever she did really horrible things to me in the past, she would only have to say 'hello' again with that smile of hers and she was forgiven. Reflecting on what happened changed my opinion of her: being her friend was a risk and I knew her too well to get sucked in, so I cut her out, loaded all the blame on to her, really.

'I wouldn't bother collecting me today 'cos it's not worth it. Please don't waste your time and ruin your day by coming over here and trying to change my mind. I'm feeling very confused at the moment and I can't take being near anyone; it's a very frightening feeling and I'm completely lost in that desert. I have no strength to fight or even cry today. Sometimes I get upset about the arguments with Dad. I know it's only an argument but it feels like he hates me. When you asked me to write about where my feelings might come from yesterday I was feeling very bitter about it all and I wrote it all down, but I left them out and they read them and that's when the shouting started. I feel kind of patchy; one moment I am fine and then suddenly I turn into a monster and come out with all these awful things.

I went for a visit to the Heritage Centre, to see what it was like. At first I didn't want to but this personal adviser person said that if I saw anyone from school, he would take us straight home. I agreed reluctantly and went. It turned out that there wasn't anyone from school there so I *had* to go in and look around. I forgot to say, the Heritage Centre is lots of ancient railway not when they were in the house. What causes irrational fear?

Some trigger experiences that have caused phobias can quite easily be identified. I am very frightened of strange dogs, particularly if they bark. In North Africa 'pie dogs' roamed the streets and they could quite literally take a small child, or attack a larger one. We were taught to be afraid of them; they were a real threat. I guess I gradually imposed this fear on all dogs and now if a dog barks at me I certainly give off the fear pheromones that will alert it to my weakness. When I owned my own dog, I remained fearful of other dogs for her sake as well as my own! The Middle East contains other scary creatures that children need to be wary of—scorpions for example – very large house spiders move rather like scorpions. I have gradually learned not to stamp on them, but to 'rescue' them with a glass and a postcard. But when a zoo warden came to see my infant class and showed them the 'friend' he had brought with him— a tarantula—I fainted! So what is this all about?

Ward (2001:19) suggests that *'a phobic person does not really know why he is afraid, any more than a person who laughs at a joke knows why he is laughing. [...] In the grip of a phobic reaction, the phobic individual exists in a peculiar state of knowing something and not knowing it at the same time.'*

In the grip of a phobic reaction, intelligence and logic are actually of no apparent use. Other people will try to convince you that what you believe is silly or without

carriages along an old platform, that have been made into proper classrooms. I met one of the people in charge and we sat with him in the catering carriage with some coffee, while I told him about my 'school phobia'. I really hate that description. He then took me alone around the site which was really nice but I was too nervous to take it all in. I met other people too and they were all friendly but I couldn't wait to leave.

Repressive behaviour between children is very very easy to disguise as childish teasing. The other problem is that when you are a kid, you don't have the right language or vocabulary to describe situations, so it's easier to say nothing. I said nothing and the problems just got compounded. I am quite a sensitive girl and as these situations went on, I lost all confidence in myself and my ability to 'turn the other cheek', to 'ignore it', to 'pull myself together'. I became a victim and I allowed my victim personality to take me over. It was just easier that way, and at the time life seemed too difficult and the easy option was to escape into myself, my bed and my pyjamas.

I fight with Steph so much at the moment. It's wrong but I take a lot out on her even though she is only just twelve years old. It scares me how angry I get with her and I hate myself for it. She sometimes provokes me but because I have been so over sensitive recently I take it way too far.

Sometimes, and only sometimes, I would get up with a boost of confidence and just go to school myself. My stubbornness to the fore, I would intend to defeat the problem by ignoring it and getting on with my life. I would be bored being at home and this was probably a driver too—I missed talking to people, having mates, laughing with friends. When I got there though there were no friends, no mates, there was no support mechanism for me and the positive moment was quickly lost.

I went quite far to get out of going to

substance. Dreams are a nightly reminder says Ward, *'that we can believe almost anything. [...] We believe in a world populated by objects and experiences that have not, will not and cannot happen in reality.'* (2001:20)

My terror of spiders prompted me to read a story about 'the spider with only 7 legs' or some such title to my infant class. The story made a mini-heroine out of a physically impaired creature whose own fear was Hoovers. A well written little tale which forced me to re-think my usual ploy of sucking up the offenders who came anywhere near my home. I began to think about them as creatures with feelings; they don't know I rationalised, that they are scary spiders. This recognition of what it would be like to be a small beast in the world of a big human really helped me.

I approached Gemma's phobia with a similar strategy. I taught her to change it into an image that could be inspected and walked around in her head. The image as has been shown in the previous chapter became 'Raef'.

This did not at first help me to identify the phobic trigger. I still did not understand why school, or any type of educational buildings could cause such a severely physical reaction in any one. What was she afraid of?—this was not nearly as easy as spiders.

A colleague of mine had a type of nervous breakdown when she was over 50. Suddenly she became agoraphobic and could not do her job as an educational adviser,

school. One day Mum had left the house to take Steph to Junior School and while she was gone, I suddenly remembered that our next-door-neighbours were on holiday and we had their key so I grabbed it and ran out of the front door. I quickly ran across our front garden to their house and went inside. Then I went upstairs and sat in one of the bedrooms. I couldn't believe that I had sunk this low and I knew it wouldn't do any good but I felt scared and didn't know where to run. I heard Mum come home into our house and she began calling for me. It did not take her long to realise where I might have gone. She came over and knocked on the front door. She told me to open it or she would call the police. At first I said no because I knew that if I did she might try to get me into school. In the end, I knew it was a bad idea and opened the door. Mum took me back home and I didn't go to school that day.

'Once when I was dragging her to school, I just thought about what was happening, having this terrible shouting match with my daughter in the street, she was screaming, I was screaming...what was going on...I couldn't recognise her; it was really terrible.'

Once I got the courage from somewhere to go to a Jubilee disco at the village hall. There were kids there from school and I found that I was able to ignore them. They did look at me but I guess that was because no-one had seen me for so long. That night when I left the hall to walk home, I cried. I felt lost and hopeless just like Jas felt in the desert. Something made it feel like a desert wind too when I was out there except without sand but it was haunting and cold. I felt freezing and my hands were numb but I didn't care. It was as if I wanted to feel bad and had forgotten what it feels like to feel good. I felt weak when I got home and I knew I would not be going to the centre the next day.

Although going to the Referral Centre helps me I sometimes feel like it's the travelling around to schools to advise on children with learning difficulties. This seemed to defy all logic, even to her. When she was in recovery we talked about what her panic attacks had looked like in comparison to Gemma's. At one stage my colleague was told that she would be having Cognitive Behaviour Therapy to help her, she wondered if it was something that was being considered for Gemma. This type of re-training actually fitted quite well into what happened at the beginning of my work with Gemma—you cannot just take away the undesirable behaviour; it would leave a void: 'stop doing that' cannot work. What you have to consider is what to replace it with. In our case it was 'investigating the effects.'

'When my girl is in her panic attack, I talk to her and get her to examine the fear—what is happening now? Can't breathe, can't breathe. I talk her down calmly and gently, all the while asking her to think about what this situation feels like...now we have progressed to her being able to say, 'I'm hyperventilating, I can't stop my hands flapping, this is silly, I can do it...I can just sit here, it's slowing down.' Talking down when the person is also describing the feelings to themselves and to you is very time consuming—on one occasion we sat in the car outside the Heritage Centre for four and a half hours. But at the end of the time she did enter the centre and have a cup of coffee with the manager. One small step for Gemma, one giant leap for us all. The next level of replacement was to make her a talisman. We spent some time talking about

only thing happening in my life. Nothing exciting ever happens. I can't remember the last time it did. I find myself getting bored and extremely lonely. I always think about what I should have done or shouldn't have done. It goes through my mind nearly every day and every night.

'Last night I had never been so bitter and twisted in my life. Not even at the worst time in year 7, so now I am starting to wonder if that is the real me coming out; maybe I am just really that bitchy and cruel inside, and this is why I'm in the position I am now.

Today I promised Lesleyann that I would pay a visit to the Heritage Centre with her to do some research. When I woke up, this horror went through me as I realised that I had the same feeling as I did on school mornings. All I did was turn over and put the covers over my head to shut the world out. This didn't work because Mum came in and told me to get up. I then moved to my next tactic of not getting dressed to stop them getting me out of the front door.

Lesleyann arrived and came into the room. As usual I sat on my bed looking awful and she took a seat next to me. She asked what I was thinking. In truth I was thinking that there was no way I was going anywhere. I couldn't actually say that though. She told me that I could just get dressed. I panicked but she said that getting dressed isn't scary. I could see her point so I got dressed, then had some tea with her and Mum. Then it was time to go and I didn't want to make a fuss in front of Lesleyann so we left. When we got there it took about four hours to get me out of the car. It sounds really sad but it's true. I would not budge and worrying about causing a stir in front of Lesleyann went out of the window. She began to ask why I had ended up like this and I told her about the things that had happened at school. Some people had made me feel stupid and got me down.

Then she said, 'Then it's about time you

the role of amulets, lucky charms and talismans. Gemma loves unusual words, magic and ancient mythology so this part was easy. She has experienced a lot of death in her short life, both of her Nans, her uncle and aunt all dying within a short space of time when she was just old enough to understand and feel the loss. So I found her an old penny which had the same date as one Nan's birth date, drilled a hole in it and threaded it onto a velvet ribbon. When she felt worried she could rub the coin to bring her Nan into her head, *'If Nan could be here it might be ok.'* This seemed bizarre but certainly worked and it got us through a few Monday mornings. She reported reaching for her coin as soon as she woke up and *'it made it ok.'* This I believe is similar to recently bereaved people holding their loved one's clothes and drawing strength from the smell— you have something of theirs to ameliorate the loss. The physical act of holding something brings a type of relief. At each session that Gemma attended at the centre her coin was prominently displayed. This lasted for quite a long time, and saw her through the most difficult parts of her recovery.

Talisman time coincided with Gemma learning about 'liminality': the threshold between trauma and recovery. What she liked best about this descriptive word was that it signalled that there was a threshold, that there could be convalescence from this awful and destructive period of her life.

Another important strategy was to have an agenda. A person going through any sort of trauma

proved them wrong.' It seemed such a simple thing to say, but it sort of worked a bit...after hours of talking I agreed to go in. All we did was sit in a room doing some of our research. What the hell was I worrying about? There isn't anything in there that can hurt me!

Depression is anger without enthusiasm. Lesleyann found this sentence somewhere and it is so true. The idea actually made me feel much more positive somehow; anger can be turned into something more creative so therefore so can depression.

I found that there were lots of different and separate groups of people in secondary school. One big group were the 'popular kids' the 'royalty group' of the school and then there were the 'nurds' who were like scum to the 'royalty' and then there were the 'really clever kids' – some were modest about their intelligence and some were really big headed about it. Then there were the 'revolutionaries' who really didn't care, they did whatever they wanted to do and had fun. So what was I? I was sort of a rebel because I didn't suck up to the popular kids, and I may have been seen as a 'nurd'. I wasn't a rebel as in being tough and breaking rules but I was comfortable being myself and didn't just do what everyone else did.

Matt hung around with some quite rough boys, I don't think he got involved with bullying but some of his mates did. One of them was Darren who had pushed me with his bike into the road. I didn't think any the less of Matt for hanging round with him because I knew he was a good person. I met him in year 7 and we'd chat in class and tease each other. I don't know why Matt was friends with them but I can only assume it was a boy thing and that being in a group like that provides people with protection—safety in numbers, I suppose.

Matt can seem tough but to my sister and me he is a lot softer and we have a laugh. Sometimes it's less pressure when it's boys and girls rather than being with loses their routine. Getting back a routine can be an important first step to re-establishing a normal life. Even having mini-routines for getting up produces a succession of small challenges that can be achieved with a feeling of satisfaction. Each feeling of satisfaction builds into a 'feel-good factor'. Gemma was in the habit of remaining in her 'rabbit pyjamas' for hours after she had awoken in the morning; mornings were not starting properly for her so it was very easy for her to drift along into the rest of the day. We worked out a small list of activities with some timings for her to achieve. At the beginning it included the talisman. This recognition of the significance of the talisman was as important as believing in the reality of the panic attacks. It is not unusual for profound fear to cause actual sickness, so that feeling ill is not a made up thing but has become a physical reality. Dismissing this as 'pretend' is to add to the feeling of invisibility, or the diminishing of the person.

The zoo warden who thought that he could 'conquer my fear' by introducing me to a tarantula in front of my class was shocked and frightened himself by the effect it had on me. I doubt he will ever do that again to anyone.

When Gemma spoke about her stomach upsets, I suggested that she tried some herbal remedies and we went out looking for particular plants with which to make infusions for her to drink. When she said she had a headache, I let her see that I believed it, many of these situations were real produced by

the same sex, where you are expected to behave in a particular way. I think we both still feel as though we can be big kids around each other. Even now when we are much older, we still tend to muck about as children would do.

I have never understood why it is like this but it seems to work. Especially now when we have to be more grown up in everyday life, it feels good just to forget about it all and have fun. It made a difference particularly when I had no friends up north.

Our first animal was Benson the cat; he was actually living there before me. Then we got rabbits. Toby first, he died the same weekend as my Dad's mum. I think I was about 5 when that happened, death as a family issue came early to me. The second rabbit was Harvey but he ran away which was horrible because we didn't know what had happened to him. Me and my sister went around putting posters on lampposts but we never discovered what had become of him. We had Charlie the cat at the same time as Toby the rabbit; they used to play together. We still have Charlie; he is big and ginger and very sleepy most of the time. He used to sleep on top of the compost heap and was constantly covered in fleas, slugs and tiny snails and regularly needed a good clean. Benson got cancer but the pills didn't work, and when my sister and I were out one day Mum and Dad had him put down because he was just going downhill and I know now that this was the right thing to do. I remember the day we were told he had cancer; we were at the vet's and Mum came out crying and sat on a bench outside and told us *'some really sad news...'*. We asked if he was going to die, and of course he did but as a child this seemed almost unreal; as I said death in our family came early to me.

When I was in year five, my Nan (my mother's Mum) died and during the same weekend my Mum's cousin aged only 47 died too. My Mum was phoned in tension and fear, and gradually the pretend versions slipped away as she recognised that they were not serving any useful purpose. Unconditional positive regard was a very very helpful stance to maintain. When I commiserated with her about an illness that had prevented her from doing something that she should have done she started to feel guilty if it had not been real, began to realise how bad it is to let people down who believe in you.

Miller (1995:64) writes that *'the depressive phases may last several weeks before strong emotions from childhood break through. It is as though the depression has held back the effect. When it can be experienced, insight and associations related to the repressed scenes follow, often accompanied by significant dreams. The patient feels fully alive again until a new depressive phase signals something new.'* Miller is writing about dramatic and traumatic incidents of childhood. She is concerned with enabling damaged 'patients' to use a creative examination of their childhood to understand more about the roots of their depression. These people are remembering incidents from long ago, but their reported memories and the way that they made sense of them at a later date has a great deal of resonance with ideas that Gemma was surfacing. In philosophising about her own situation, trying herself to make sense of the way that people had acted towards her, and her interpretations of those actions. Linking interpretation to a situation allowed her to realise for herself her own misconceptions

the middle of the night about my Nanna, who had been taken to hospital with apparent asthma. This may have been what we were told as children. She was in hospital for quite a long time, but she had cancer and so this night she had died in her sleep. While our family were reeling from the shock of that, my Mum had been told about her cousin. My Mum told my sister and me that Nanna had gone to heaven and so had her cousin. *'I've got some really sad news for you...'* I knew what that meant. I went on a school trip on the Monday: Mum said that it was what Nanna would have wanted me to do. I wasn't sure about attending the funeral, I think I did the right thing and yes, I do think that Nanna would have wanted me to go. I wrote a poem about Nanna and Mum used it for the funeral.

'I'm scared that I would not have been able to tell you all this face to face, so I thought this letter would be better than not letting you know at all and leaving you to come and find me like I am now. I am not in a state, I just don't know who I am any more, believe me this is not just an excuse. Did I ever tell you that I always have these bad thoughts especially at night about everything that happened to me? Sometimes I think about it too much so the next day I'm exhausted. I feel ill and drained out all of the time. Last year it was so bad that I felt weak and I nearly fell over quite a bit. On Sunday I felt weak and I did fall. I felt very down that night. Steph is home today so I don't want a fuss, but I don't mind if you want to come and talk about this letter. I'm scaring myself and have restless sleep every night with bad dreams.'

When my mum's friend was asking me about the Heritage Centre it felt as if she was asking me more out of pity (Oh, poor thing she can't cope with school so she has to do this instead). But I reckon that she was just worried 'cos she is really nice.

When I first started at the Referral Centre I felt a lot different. I was very depressed and the over stated drama with which she had imbued events. '*I think now I see what I was doing.*' Furedi (2004:119) has suggested that '*People are encouraged to see themselves as victims rather than self-determining agents...How and what people remember is influenced by their predicament.*'

Gemma was angry about what had happened to her but that anger had dissipated into a self-centred melancholic phobia that was destructive.

One of Miller's (1995:68) clients stated that '*It was not the beautiful or pleasant feelings that gave me new insight, but the ones against which I had fought most strongly: feelings that made me experience myself as shabby, petty, mean, helpless, humiliated, demanding, resentful or confused; and above all, sad and lonely. It was precisely through these experiences, which I had shunned for so long, that I became certain that I now understood something about my life, stemming from the core of my being that I could not have learned from any book.*'

Most importantly now, Gemma had to take control of her own destiny and get beyond a counselled and supported situation. Bentley (1998:85) rightly states:

'*If you want to change your future only you can do it.*'

but now I feel much better and I think it is because I am getting out during the week and learning things at the same time. Now I have something to discuss with people; I have things that I have done to relate to my family—I have a bit more of a life. I don't yet have mates, but I do have activities and achievements, I do have something to talk about.

A week ago was my review of my time at the Referral Centre. I was nervous about going to it but I am glad that I did because it turned out to be very positive. Everyone said that I was doing well which I was relieved to hear and they asked me if I would like to stay on until the summer holidays. I think this is because they wanted me to keep feeling confident and it would be too soon for me to stop just yet. I must admit that at the moment, there actually feels like there is a light at the end of the tunnel.

Everyone I am working with at the moment makes me feel that I matter, that I wasn't just being stupid and that my problems were actually real ones that needed to be sorted.

'What children most wanted from adults, Stella remembered, was to matter, to be liked for themselves.' (North Patterson, 2000:274)

Mum's got a thing on the wall: 'Your friend is the person who knows everything about you and still likes you.'

The adviser looked me straight in the eye and asked if I honestly thought that I would ever go back to school. I said 'no' pretty much straight away. What was great was that he asked me. I wasn't sure what we were going to be able to do about this but he took note of what I had said, my voice was being heard.

CHAPTER FOUR

Childhood
A Terminal Crisis

The Betrayal of Trust

When you are researching, or even merely interested in a subject, something almost magical happens. You begin to notice 'useful material' in every printed paper you read; the words you are using to write suddenly appear in poignant songs; someone rings you about a related issue even though they didn't know about your research. Your brain is subconsciously tuned in to noticing any detail that concerns your subject area even in the most unlikely places. I have always been aware of this phenomena but never more so than when working on this project.

'The child must forget past hopes and wishes, while his exuberant imagination is tamed and harnessed to the laws of impersonal things.' (Erikson, 1963:258)

Gemma wrote some of her earliest memories of school at the very beginning of our project. Quite recently I read a magazine article written by the model Penny Lancaster and felt the hair stand up on the back of my neck. Penny was describing her own bullied school days and the words she used were almost identical to those used by Gemma.

'I think at school you have to blend in and be the same as everybody else...I was picked on for being different.'

On my first day of school, I remember standing in the playground with Mum and Steph who was also wearing a school dress. She actually wasn't starting school that day but because I was she wore my spare pinafore. No-one argued with her so there she stood in clothes two years too big for her. We must have looked really odd as I probably brought George the Gnome along (I had grown attached to George when I was very young; I took him everywhere and we used to keep him by the back door in our old house). I was slightly overwhelmed as there were loads of other kids with their Mum's and Dad's too.

My teacher was lovely; she had soft dark brown curly hair, brown eyes and olive skin. I always liked her skirts; she wore bangles down her arms and pretty rings on her fingers. I decided that I liked her straight away as she looked after me when Mum and Steph headed home.

I don't remember much about the actual lessons. I remember sitting at a desk with a couple of girls and probably boys. Anyway we all had a little break sitting at these little plastic tables drinking juice and nibbling biscuits, which I enjoyed. I started to feel more relaxed by then. I didn't talk to my future friends until a little later on in the first term. There was, though, a girl that I liked despite not even knowing her at all. Anyway I wanted to get to know her and kept going over and saying things, I also smiled at her from my table but never got one back. Eventually she gave me a chance and we stayed friends until the end of junior school but throughout that time I think she thought I was odd. I probably was, she may even have been a bit scared

'The bullying would be anything from throwing rubbers, teasing me in class to following me home and taunting me on the journey. I remember a couple of girls used to get this friend of theirs to ram his bike up the back of my legs.'

'The bullying didn't happen all the time but enough that it made an impact on my future life and the way I feel about things. I was a very nervous, anxious person at school. If I read to the class I'd always worry what other people would think—whether I was going to be good enough or if someone was going to laugh at me.'

Looking back at the previous chapter I find all of these ideas reiterated almost precisely in Gemma's words. When a young woman at my college was left sitting outside the classroom having just rushed from her lesson, it was clear to me that she was being bullied. I used the ideas I had gleaned from Gemma to talk to her, to get her into a comfortable position where she was understood rather than 'comforted', and in this way to get her to open up to me about how she was perceiving what was happening to her:

'Are these girls the popular ones, like royalty at the school, do you feel that you are not one of the popular kids?'
'Mmm.'

'It was probably especially difficult when you came back after being away; did you feel like a bit of an outsider, they had all done things that you didn't know about?'
'I used to have a friend so it didn't

of me too.

I was shy at infant school, believe it or not, but I didn't care about what people thought of me. I just wish I could still feel that now. I had lots of fun in that school and continued being friends with people I met there for a long time. I liked my first day at school, plus it seemed like a bonus that I didn't feel scared but happy and care free. I had nothing to worry about at all. Well, all except who to be partners with when you had to hold hands with someone who might just have been picking their nose!

When I was 12 my best subjects were English and Drama. I would have liked art more but it seemed so restrictive; they told us what to do and we couldn't really use our imaginations freely. In the mornings I would come into school and meet my friends in the playground. We would sit on the same bench and talk about anything, bitch about people, what lessons we were going to have, the fact that we hadn't done our homework and then we would hear the bell ring and we would walk to our form room for registration. By that time I had met my best two friends and we used to hang around together. When we got to the form room we would race to our table because it was a two seater table with an odd seat at the end and none of us liked to be on that odd chair. Surprisingly the teacher never told us off for doing that but then we were at the back and all the loud boys were at the front keeping the teacher's attention. When the register was called we would sometimes miss our names because we were showing each other pictures in magazines, but it was good to have friends to share things with. So what went wrong with that...?

Suddenly these girls became 'girly' and I was made to feel stupid. I had always been one to speak my mind and this used to be OK, but now they blanketed everything with innuendo. They stopped being natural, it was all an act. This has affected me even now. I still don't speak matter that I wasn't part of the popular group, I had someone to hang around with, but then I was away; it was different when I came back, she had gone over to them.'

'What is it about you that they think is different?'
'I don't come from round here, they say I talk different.' She looked at me then with startled eyes and said: 'How did you know it was about that stuff?'

We started to talk about her life and her ambitions, her hopes and fears and she stopped sobbing.

In order to help children who are experiencing something less than a carefree childhood, we first have to accept that we do not as adults understand that childhood. The lives of children today bear almost no resemblance to the lives that most of the adults around them experienced; more than at any other time in history there is very little shared experience between children and adults. Children today know things and expect things that were only ever the domain of adults in the past. This has affected how they react to situations and who they do or do not turn to in times of crisis. Children learn quite quickly how to manipulate adults; and that there are different expectations of behaviour in different contexts. What has changed incrementally and is now almost out of control is that even very young children have no awe of adults. Partly this has arisen because there are now very few things that are sacrosanct to an adult state; children are allowed to and indeed expect

my mind really. I'm starting to get better with some people but I am definitely not open with my peers in the way that I once was. I always wonder how they will accept what I want to say, and so end up not saying it, 'just in case'.

I was really happy as we were, me and a couple of close friends and a few acquaintances but they wanted to really fit into the second level popular group. I was off school again—I wonder why! My special friend didn't have me to hang around with so she had got more involved with the others and when I came back I felt like an outsider.

When we were young my sister and I played at 'radio stations'. Mum would often be the 'special guest'. We had an ordinary tape-recorder and we used a tape that we didn't need any more, putting sticky tape over the lock hole so that it would record. Then we would invent a little 'jingle' at the beginning of the 'programme' to introduce the show and we did competitions, interviews and the news and weather. Whenever we wanted a song, then we would turn up the real radio and record a song from there. Sometimes we would even write our own songs. One of our favourites was called 'Granny's Grotto' with reggae music for the background.

My younger sister Steph is dark haired like my Dad and she has lovely olive skin that gives her a European look too, just like him. She is infuriatingly pretty with wonderful deep dark eyes and long dark eye lashes; in fact if she wasn't so nice I could really hate her! Somehow she is a sort of unity of brother and sister: she would always take the male part in our games. She is a beautiful 'tomboy' and we loved playing 'Power Rangers' – she was always Zac the Red Ranger and I was always Trinny the Yellow Ranger. We loved 'He-Man', 'Postman Pat' and 'Pingu' on TV. Steph was always fearless and has continued to be a very outdoor girl. She used to have hospitals for slugs and snails and farms for woodlice and many adult experiences. Whilst I would not advocate fear as a way of controlling children, when the adult has no ranking position their authority is entirely and crucially dependent on personality and on the extent to which they are able to 'charm' the child. Charming a class of children is nigh on impossible. The decline of giving adults a title (Mrs, Miss, Auntie, Officer, Sir), appears to be in direct proportion to the decline in discipline on a more general level.

'Caning was normal, caning was the admittance by the teacher that they had lost control of a person in the class, and that person was sent for the cane, they controlled the class by fear and violence. I am not sure what education ever did for me, I fought it, hated it, and yet I was there every day.'

'Parenting involves many processes: welcoming, caring, guiding, teaching, protecting, introducing the child into the family and the wider world. It means communicating values, ways of seeing, ways of thinking, ways of being. It means supporting children's activities and desires, containing them, accepting their differences from us, tolerating what we find difficult. Above all it means respecting the child...' (Orbach, 2001:105-6)

Most children have more material things than their grandparents ever dreamed of and many that didn't even exist when their parents and grandparents were children. There is actually very little to 'look forward to' about being an adult apart from debt and frustration. Work is seen as 'toil' rather than

ladybirds but she is terrifid of blood! She is not as tomboyish now but there is still a bit there. She is, though, the peacemaker of the family and she sticks up for everyone, but her black moods can be devastating and we all run from those! She is always able to make me laugh, partly because we have exactly the same bizarre sense of humour; we can look at each other in some situations and know exactly what we are thinking and what we mean by a gesture. I could have talked to her about school but she was way too young to understand what I was feeling at the time. More recently she has been much more understanding and very very supportive. But that is because we are close and she still partly takes the role of defender.

My Drama teacher was really nice. She had freckles and strawberry blonde hair which was shoulder length. She was probably mid-twenties so quite newly qualified, but she stood up for herself even though she was young and most people liked her lessons and enjoyed themselves . She was shocked by the change in my personality when I was able to become someone else in a drama situation. I was normally quite shy and quiet in class, but 'in-character' I could be loud and brash. In short I could be 'someone else'; pity I couldn't do that in other situations!

My Science teacher used to help me to catch up with my work after I had time off. I think he tried to understand but wasn't really given any time to do so. He was young with a northern accent. He had heaps of patience and taught by walking round the class, seeing how everyone was doing and helping those who were stuck so that you didn't need to put your hand up every time you were unsure. I can see now that this was very supportive of weaker students and also stopped anyone else knowing what you needed help with. There was no disruption in his lessons; we all just got on with our work knowing he was walking round to help.

any type of vocation, and there is nothing much left to aim for since most of the equipment that you might want as an adult you will have already been given as a child.

"I would never have done this to my parents— kids were more in awe of their parents than they are now, all this answering back, not just a bit of lip really strong stuff. Disobedience wasn't tolerated, there was a line that would just never be crossed—the language that kids use now, it just wouldn't have been accepted in the past.'

'Her grandparents thought it would be seen as plain truancy—there is now such a lack of respect, I just couldn't imagine doing this to my mother, it wasn't about fear, just something that you didn't do.'

'I was letting her down, a parent should be able to make things better.'

'I was angry that she wasn't being normal and just going to school. I couldn't always talk to my friends about it; they all had normal children who went off to school every day, they sympathised but I could tell that they didn't really understand what was going on and sometimes didn't know how to talk to me about it.'

'She was so confident as a baby, she loved primary school. When it all happened I just thought where has all this come from?—it was just totally out of control. She was split up from her friend and this clearly had an impact on her—they said that it was because she was

My form tutor was in his mid thirties and I generally liked him except when he was in a bad mood. He offered to talk to me about my problems but I don't think I did. This is a difficult thing to do. If you go to talk to the teacher two things might happen: the kids would get to know that you had done it and would take it out on you more; or they would see you as befriending a teacher and this is perceived as being a 'swot'.

'The wounds of childhood, because they were harder to comprehend, lingered. They could not be healed by reason.' (Richard North Patterson, 2002:242).

I remember one time in particular. It was a really horrible morning and everything seemed to go wrong. My Mum out of desperation could not think of any way to get me to school other than by physically dragging me up the road. I can't remember how she got me to dress into my school uniform but somehow I did. After that she had to almost push me down the stairs. At the time I was hysterical and completely out of control. I was not acting or feeling like me at all and although I was really scaring myself, the thought of school scared me even more. This was in suburbia by the way so plenty of people probably saw us but neither Mum nor I cared or noticed. I cried and tried to pull away from her but it didn't work. In the end, to my horror we were walking through those dreaded school gates and into reception and even worse the Head of Year was just there staring at us. Mum explained briefly what had happened but this teacher didn't say a word; she just took hold of my arm and marched me towards assembly. I remember that as I slipped away from Mum I started to beg her not to let this happen, and she began to cry. I felt so sorry for her and so guilty. I still feel that way even now when it is six years later. Neither of us got any words of comfort and I hate to think that she walked down the road all alone.
The Head of Year 7 was hateful. She had long red hair and a high pitched

quiet and the friend was confident, they said it would 'do Gemma good'. I wasn't told about it until it happened, wasn't consulted at all.'

'All this went on too long; we had no support from the school, they just sent 'standard' letters with my name written on the top. They obviously went to all parents of children who had been absent lots of times. There was no acknowledgement that this was developing into a 'situation.'

'The pressure was on the parents to 'sort this out before 8.30am. There was no recognition of the impact that this might be having on a family.The worst situation was when I had to drag her along the street and we were screaming at each other and I just wondered what was happening to us. No-one helped me with this at the school.'

'You were always holding your breath even when she did go in. Her mood could change on a Sunday and you could see it happening. Then sometimes she would just get up and go. Parents don't really know how to talk to a child; they feel alone with a problem that seems to have been caused by them but they don't know how. I had let her down and I couldn't deal with the problem—I was desperate about being a failed parent.'

'The scenes in the mornings were the worst, I tried saying, "We are saying these things because we love you, not because we hate you." It didn't work.'

'She feels definitely that school let

screechy voice; nobody liked her. She was probably in her early forties and wore frumpy clothes; she was quite bony so all her clothes hung on her thin frame. When you don't like someone do you only see the worst aspects of them? She was the least understanding person I had met up to that time, and she certainly did not appear to like or understand teenagers. The only kids who came close to being liked by her were the brainy ones. She liked pupils who made the school look good; she wanted to sweep problems under the carpet and pretend they didn't exist. She was probably very relieved when I left the school to move to the North. Her best effort on my behalf was 'we'll keep an eye on you.' I didn't notice this happening or really understand what she meant by it. Certainly nothing changed. I think that she had told the rest of the staff about me, because if I reported 'sick' to the office, I was always referred back to her.

Claxton (1990:151) states: *'Pupils' stances in schools are "solutions" to the problem of how best to be, in a predicament that includes motivational, emotional, personal, social and cultural ingredients, as well as cognitive ones. A teacher may play a leading or insignificant role in this predicament.'*

I never had any meetings with the Headteacher. He was a distant figure in my early secondary school life in the South. I believe that he instructed the Deputy Head to send letters to my home suggesting that I wasn't attending enough. By contrast the Headteacher of my new secondary school in the North spoke to me often during my limited attendance at his school and he certainly knew who I was. I am now aware that he actively supported my 'alternative' provision at the Heritage Centre and was always asking about my progress.

When you are a kid I think that you believe that the Head-teacher is the *her down, not her parents, she feels a lot of hatred for the school. It was all short term measures; nothing was resolved at all. There is no-one in a school with a dedicated role to deal with this sort of thing—no-one who can act as a proper counsellor; regular teachers just don't have time.'*

'We just couldn't get through, there was no communication; it was really frustrating, we couldn't get through at all, not to them, not to her.'

'The main argument in favour of an early return to school appears to be that continued absence creates secondary complications such as falling behind in school work, losing contact with friends and exposure to the secondary gain of remaining at home. It is claimed that the longer a child remains out of school, the more anxious he becomes and the stronger the dependency between parent(s) and the child becomes. Rodriques (*et al* 1959) found that an early return to school helped the school phobic children under 11 years of age but not those who were older.' (Valles & Oddy, 1984)

'In school when I was a teenager in Germany it was more a kind of mobbing; afterwards I became quite tall and had some friends in gangs so nobody really wanted to get in trouble with me or my friends. But this is exactly the problem— you have to get in a gang to get some peace. You have to play the big tough guy to protect yourself.'

'Although I am a manager of an educational establishment now I

person who is there for you when things go wrong, that they have the time to spend talking to you and sorting things out. A Headteacher is a parent figure to a child and it's very disappointing when they seem not to want to take on that mantle. The only Head-teacher that I remember with any sense of comfort is the Head of the infant school who was warm and motherly and knew all the children by name. I had a good time at Infant school.

I remember a time when Mum and I would sit at our kitchen table listening to all the different experts' opinions on the matter. We would sometimes feel positive after the discussions but it wouldn't last for long because nothing really changed. At the end of the day they all wanted me to go back to school, but to me this was the reason why this had happened in the first place. I felt trapped because I had no choices. It was either home or school. At home I watched a lot of TV: it was better and more interesting than real life—well my life anyway.

I had quite a lot of time off in year 7. No one seemed to help me so my family and I felt very alone. The fact that I kept having time off made me stand out so people would start going on about it and ask why. I just said I was ill but I don't think they believed me. I got more and more short tempered and snapped at people who got on my nerves and started to moan and worry a lot more than I used to. Some were surprised to see this side of me because they all thought that I was quiet but when I was with friends I was mad and always laughing. I felt uncomfortable in the end because some girls who had been friends kept pushing me away and saying funny things to make me feel unwelcome and stupid. Then my best friend met this other girl and started doing everything with her which upset me and got me angry. I had been friends with her for years and suddenly I was forgotten. Another girl tried to help me patch things up but we would always end up arguing with each hated school and that was probably due to the fact that I was made to feel inadequate. Looking back, my father was a high achiever and because I was dyslexic he couldn't understand the way dyslexic people learn, no-one did then.. I was sent to a private school and they made me feel inadequate and stupid.'

'It was just life...I accepted it although I didn't like it. Lots of days I was frightened by the regime, I've never been big but I wasn't bullied; there were strategies that I used, there were a couple of fights and I was a fighter. Once you have fought someone hard you don't get bullied...they will pick on someone who doesn't fight back or can't fight back. At about 13 my eyes started to go...no-one else noticed and this was something else. I knew that I couldn't see but no one noticed. If I had been more sensible I would have told somebody because I knew I couldn't see but I didn't want to admit it, because that might mean that I wouldn't be able to do the things that I wanted to do...but then I couldn't play sport properly and there was less and less that I could do.'

'What kids like Gemma have to know is that everyone has some sort of fear, even grown ups have fears. This is not just something that has happened to her, these things happen to other people; they just deal with it differently.'

other which made it worse. Through these two years at school we were both always friends deep down but other people and problems got in the way. We both changed and although I still cared about her I wasn't sure that we would ever be the same.

Year 8 was better. I attended school a lot more, partly because I missed my friends and partly I had got a bit more brave about facing up to people who were nasty to me. Certain people, one boy in particular, stopped having a go at me and showed more respect after I stood up to them.

My family had decided that we wanted to move from Essex to Cumbria. My last day of school in Essex was great fun and loads of people signed a card and my school shirt, which I still have now. We packed up the car with our three cats and four rabbits then left our well loved home. I had lived in Essex all my life but now we were going to a completely different place that hardly anyone has ever heard of. My previous school had over 1500 pupils, the new one probably had no more than 700—it was bound to be ok here, wasn't it?

I am not sure if people believed me when I said I was ill. I don't think that they thought about it much. They all had their own problems. I just wish that I had realised this at the time. That I am not the only one who gets scared and has hang-ups; lots of people do. Some of them hide problems, some run away from them but in the end none of this works, you have to cope and deal with it, look at your life honestly and ask if you are really happy and if not, then do something about it. Don't let others control the way that your life goes: bullies are controllers if you let them. They walk away after and get on with their lives; you are left in the shreds of yours.

CHAPTER FIVE

Victimisation:
The diminishing person

Will 'o' the Wisp

In the popular press, one of the most common subjects for 'agony aunts' is that related to self esteem, for example:

'Every year my self-esteem plummets even lower. Now I hate myself so much that I wish I was dead. I suffered cruel put-downs and racist abuse as a teenager. This has made me very wary of trying to talk to people, and I am unable to establish friendships or relationships. I need some practical help. I don't want to talk to a doctor or counsellor because they tend to be judgemental or dismissive.'
(Mail, February 2003)

So in terms of 'baggage' young people come to a clinical psychology centre with all sorts of difficulties and I'm looking ahead to your next question: 'What is your understanding of school phobia?' I could probably give you a textbook definition but I am not sure how helpful that is, because children who come with school attendance problems come for all sorts of different reasons and often the school non-attendance, either school refusal or whatever we want to call it, is just the tip of the iceberg. It's like a metaphor really: it may be disguising an extreme social anxiety – that's very common and for whatever reason kicks in at adolescence or the transition from primary to secondary. It may

'I am of course a perfect victim, I don't retaliate and anything that is said to me affects me deeply. Everything that is said to me seems to have lots of extra meanings. I always think that what happens is my fault: that's what they want, to put me down. I feel small, pathetic and pitied, and I go unnoticed. I don't have a voice; to want a voice isn't much unless you don't have one.'

Once I remember that I was refusing to go to school again on a particular morning. It was too late to catch the bus so Dad had to take me there himself even though he was supposed to be at a meeting. Anyway he managed to get me into the car (I can't remember how) and drove me down to school. We stopped a short way away because I was crying. He tried to talk to me instead of getting angry and I told him that I was scared because I thought I was going mad. After a nice chat he drove on towards the school but I refused to get out of the car. He threatened to bring the Headmaster out to get me. In the end he did go and get someone – it was the Deputy Head – and she coaxed me out of the car by saying that we would just go to her office and have a talk. Deep down I knew that I would end up trapped into staying there, but I went because I had no choice. The Deputy told me that I should stay in school for the rest of the day. I can't remember the rest of the conversation and this is probably because I have had so many just like it. I did what she asked and I stayed but I don't think I enjoyed it much at all.

In the end panic attacks in the mornings and staying at home became actually disguise a more intra-psychic problem like a depression or some sort of anxiety related to something going on in the family.

'Most people think that agoraphobia is a fear of wide open spaces. In fact it's a fear of having a panic attack when something terrible will happen. Agoraphobics react by retreating from their fear, in a bid to stop things happening. That reinforces the way that they feel, and then it spreads to become a constant seeking of safety. We don't really know what causes panic attacks. It can be a mixture of bad luck and adverse life events making you feel especially vulnerable.' (Professor Salkovskis—Mail on Sunday 2006)

'We have talked about self-determination a bit; the day unit nursing programme helps with expressing themselves in a group, assertiveness and making these links between thoughts, feelings and reflection. It's hard to be your own person, isn't it (shared laughter) if you are 13 or 14. *But it is the key to the door isn't it...once you are your own person then no-one can touch you in the way that they could before...*That's right, it can't be taken away.'

'In order to know what we wish to do next [...] we need to know ourselves, who we are and how we came to be that way.' (Craft, 1996:159)

4-19 marks a crucial phase in young people's lives. It is the period when they build on their earlier learning and prepare for adult life and employment. Many young people make this transition well—but too many do not. Too many young

more frequent. It wasn't long until I wasn't going in at all and I think I only managed about three weeks of school during that year. For the rest of it I was at home with Mum. This put a huge strain on the whole family because as far as we knew school was the only option; without that I had no future!

During my time at home, I became extremely reclusive and lived like a ghost. My Dad started calling me Will 'o' the Wisp. There were so many arguments in the family but most were between my Dad and me. We said awful things to each other and what made it worse was that neither of us would back down. I hated it but I didn't know how to make things right again. It was a horrible situation because we lost the unity between us all. Having said that, I feel like I had a lot of time with Mum and I can see now that I got to know her as a person rather than just 'Mum'.

Sometimes I was made to have little visits to school. This was part of the plan to get me used to it so that I would be ready to go back in year 10. I did go back to do my options year. It was weird seeing my old class again. I was late for registration because I had to have a 'chat' with the Deputy so I was the last person in there. When I walked in I swear the room went silent! Everyone stared at me as I walked over to my seat trying not to catch anyone's eye, but even at the time I thought it was funny. I managed to stay until Christmas. I knew subconsciously that I would leave the situation before I had chance to spoil it, but walking away effectively ruined it anyway. It didn't feel safe being happy because I felt that it would be taken away. I don't know whether this is right but maybe it had something to do with losing close family members at a young age. They were taken from us and there was nothing we could do about it. It was worrying because there were a lot of deaths, one after the other. We didn't know who was going to die next and people lose interest in learning before the age of 16. As a result fail to reach their full potential.' (DfES, 2003 '14-19 Opportunity & Excellence'). Gemma said, 'I did not lose interest in learning, I just could not do any learning in school, school became a place that I just could not be. I wanted to learn, wanted to get on but the barriers I had created between me and school were too much. It wasn't just that I had built a wall, the wall was topped with razor wire.'

'People's beliefs about their abilities have a profound effect on those abilities.' (Bandura, in Goleman 1998:90)

'To the degree that our emotions get in the way of or enhance our ability to think or plan, to pursue training for a distant goal, to solve problems and the like, they define the limits of our capacity to use our innate mental abilities, and so determine how we do in life. And to the degree to which we are motivated by feelings of enthusiasm and pleasure in what we do—or even by an optimal degree of anxiety—they propel us to accomplishment. It is in this sense that emotional intelligence is a master aptitude, a capacity that profoundly affects all other abilities, either facilitating or interfering with them.' (Goleman, 1996:80)

Bullying *victims*, that is an interesting one because as a clinical psychologist I think very often it's the children who are transferring from junior to secondary school. It's a very common reason for the refuser but the bullying is quite hidden and the child is coming home

when it was going to occur. Suddenly bad things did not seem so impossible because they did actually happen and that is the sort of thing that no one can change. I don't believe that this had a direct impact on my school life but some fears stay with you at the back of your mind. I was scared of losing control and so when I did find myself relaxing and maybe being happy for a moment I just couldn't handle it.

There was one girl who I didn't like in that school. She and her friend would sit in class and choose someone to stare at for as long as possible. They would also whisper to each other and then look at people with horrible grins on their faces. I don't remember whether she did this to me but she was out to stir things up. She kept asking awkward questions like 'Where were you last week?' 'I was ill.' 'Where were you last year?' 'I was ill.' My friends knew what she was up to before I did and knew what sort of person she was so they told me to ignore her when they overheard the conversation.

I hated the fact that I was stuck with these people in my face every day. Everybody had to fit into these rules, rules that weren't ever written or talked about. They were just there. People who couldn't let themselves be seen socialising with certain (not cool) kids. There were others who were just out to make particular individuals feel bad in order to boost their ego.There were those who sucked up shamelessly to groups that were 'high up' - what for? We were all the same species but there were so many barriers between us. This doesn't just happen at school, it can happen at work and in social networks. People are made to feel inferior because of things like being different, their appearances, having less money or flashy items. I don't want to be a part of that so I just did my own thing.

Certain kids hated me and I took pleasure in hating them back. It was fun in some ways because I wasn't in this and saying, 'I'm being bullied,'and everyone tries hard to see and to understand what is going on and they don't see it – it's the glance, it's the comment out of the side of the mouth, that actually destroys a child and which the adults don't see as a problem even if they see it at all.And our role then becomes one of helping a child to develop a suit of armour, really, to deal with what can't be stopped.

I can think of one young person in particular whose school refusal was nothing to do with bullying but related to something that was going on with a parent that we were unaware of for a long time; and maybe even the child was actually only dimly aware of. This only became apparent to everybody when the parent was admitted to hospital. I suppose that the child was sensing that something was wrong within the family, which made her feel a need to stay at home, she didn't really know why... *which is a lot for a child to take on board mentally...* yes and I would say that this is probably quite common, something happening to the child that it is less to do with school and more to do with home... *with behaviour showing at school.*

The first course of action for us (*clinical psychology centre*) is to interview the young person with their family and if it's a teenager where possible we would always talk to them on their own as well at that first interview. I personally rarely interview parents on their own having kicked the young person out of the room; I just don't think that's appropriate. Although at some stage in the treatment we

trap of having to be nice to them. It was a sort of stress relief when I said what I wanted to say to them in person. It's a bit confusing because I only stood up for myself against a few of them. I don't know why I didn't with some of the others even when they made me feel angry. I suppose that sometimes I didn't know what to say. My mind would go blank and so I just ignored them. My best friend's new friends really confused me because they weren't rude or nasty in an obvious way but I just knew that they didn't like me. This is not me being paranoid. They said weird things that had a hint of bitchiness and sarcasm behind them. They would sometimes joke with me and then say things behind my back which I occasionally heard. I didn't say anything to them though and I really don't know why. I don't like causing agro and plus they were friends with my best friend so maybe I didn't want to hurt her—this is now a long time ago; it gets a bit hazy when I think back and anyway I have moved on so this sort of thing doesn't affect me now.

Some kids can be intimidating and I have never liked confrontation so maybe that's why I didn't fight back with them. Also I never really knew where I stood with them so perhaps I wasn't angry enough and actually more confused, I was becoming less and less sure of myself because I felt that everyone was against me. It felt like mind games all the time – who was with me and who was against me: boys, girls, friends, the popular group, some teachers. It became harder and harder to feel comfortable with anyone because I never knew if they were sincere or whether they had hidden agendas.

Deep down I thought that if I controlled which people I got to know, then I wouldn't get hurt. If I pushed them away or never let them into my life in the first place, then there was no chance of losing them. It seemed better to get rid of them myself rather than them leaving might see parents on their own we don't exclude young people... *that sort of adds to their problems....*yes, it adds to the fantasy that there is something mysteriously wrong.

We always try to see young people in the family context because that is how we try to understand the problem because I think it's fair to say that whatever has caused this sort of problem to arise in the first place the chances are that the problem is maintained to some extent by the way in which people organise themselves around it, by their response to it. It's really important for us to get a sense of how parents feel and what they are doing and I think it is probably fair to say that a lot of the time when the young people themselves, either can't because they don't know or can't because it's difficult to talk to adults, say what's worrying them. I think people find that hard to understand, particularly teachers find that hard to understand actually, *to an adult it seems that if you tell me what is wrong I can maybe sort it out but that isn't what it's like to a child, it isn't as simple as 'I will tell you what's wrong' because sometimes they are not sure what's wrong.* They are not because they are overwhelmed by the sense of dread or fear and that's it.

'For me it's about masking the things you are frightened of to the world but I don't mask them to myself; I don't think anybody really knows our deepest fears, the ones we keep to ourselves; even my wife and she is my best friend, she doesn't really know my inside me, my inner person. Having some fear me or being taken away from me. This is a very lonely way to live and let me say that I don't do this any more. I wouldn't recommend it to anyone. It seemed vital back then because I had no control of anything else and it probably wasn't the best time to try and have friends, as I needed to sort my head out. There was no way that I could move on without doing that first so in a way I'm glad that I left, otherwise I wouldn't have enjoyed those friendships properly.

I never went back to that school again and I thought I would end up having this dull empty life. It was lonely back at home and all I did was hope for something better than what I had. I felt a bit cheated because my old friends down South were all doing so well but I had nothing. I felt depressed and I looked it too. My Mum said I was always tired and pale looking and that my hair had started to look really dull. She said that when I was happy it was brighter and there was life in my face.

There was a man who was trying to help us (one of the 'experts' I guess) and he suggested that I had another little visit to the school—I don't think they really knew what to do about me but they felt that they had to do something! On the appointed day I got more and more worried. I snuck out of the door and ran along the path that follows the beck at the back of our house. I climbed to the top of the bank and sat in the hollow of a tree. I remember that the helm was blowing that day (apparently according to the locals it only happens in our area and somewhere in Peru!.) It is a really strong wind that howls through the villages along the Pennines. I could not believe that I was sitting outside in this gale. It got a bit scary at some point and I ended up crying. Suddenly my dog came running towards me out of nowhere and I was so glad to see her. My Mum had gone out with her to look for me and the dog had heard me and run off to find me, then Mum couldn't find either of us. A sod of a day all round seems to be a normal condition.'

'Some of the most confident and articulate people I have met do reveal that they have these sorts of fears, and I think that it would help children to know that. However it may also be important to expose them to the idea that whatever they are feeling now won't go away; they will just learn how to deal with it as they grow up...that's what gets better.' She has a sense of that... when we were talking about general things to do with feelings that adults have about various things, debt, families, work, she said, *'Oh, it doesn't get any easier then?'*

I don't think teachers particularly (and I am speaking as one!) give any credence to the time it takes for young people like Gemma to put words around these feelings; it's not as easy as an adult explaining their feelings. I think it is often hard for grown-ups as well, isn't it?. Certainly the people who are well able to understand what children in Gemma's position are experiencing are those who have suffered from anxiety themselves or had panic attacks or whatever –when people talk about 'nameless dread', they know.

I think that part of our job really is to help young people to make these links between thoughts and feelings and behaviour and just as important is to help their parents to understand those links as well. *And give them (young people) some vocabulary to maybe think how to put this into words. I think for most people of Gemma's age they haven't got the sort of words to use; they don't know how to describe*

and yet again I was to blame. Needless to say I didn't go for the school visit and I think it was one of the last times that we saw this man. I must have frightened him off!

Some panic attacks made me feel like I couldn't breathe so I would hyperventilate which would make things worse. Afterwards I always felt ill and tired.

When I went back to the new school one time, I was just trying, it didn't mean that the fear had gone and I was OK again, I was really trying to get back to 'normal'. I must have been acting too well, and I did really need more support, not teachers and kids saying, 'Hi, haven't seen you for a while.' That really singles you out and now I see that it was just someone being kind and noticing me but it just doesn't feel like that at the time. People need to just know not to pick you out but to be 'normal' with you, that's really what you want when you are trying to get back and fit in. Fitting in, that's crucial to kids, you don't want to be 'that girl who has been ill or something.'

Up until recently I felt like my life had been stuck in a freeze frame. I still only knew the same people as I did before my problems started. Then suddenly I was getting birthday cards from new friends and everything felt like it had started moving again.

Talking things through with someone, things that adults don't normally talk about, like their own worries dreads and weaknesses, that shows you something which is both comforting and realistic. It's not easier being a grown up than being a child, it's just different and you have slightly more control over things than you do when you are a child but you still have worries, fears and responsibilities. I suppose that when you are older you don't have to worry so much about what people think and perhaps you have more time to work on *these things because that is not a vocabulary that they are used to.* No, no it's not.

One of the things that came out that she felt had happened at school is that she is quite a deep thinking person and so when she was asked questions she would be thinking of a quite complicated answer and she couldn't think of a way to explain it quickly enough and then she would be passed by – and if that happens often enough then you stop trying and I think in some lessons she just felt that 'I don't want to answer because I can't think of the words quickly enough.' Yes and then you withdraw and get a reputation and then...*people say, it's no good asking Gemma because she's never got anything to say...*It's as if there is no time to reflect.

The reflection time is getting lost in school because of the pressure to complete targets. The time for the kids or even the teacher to give them more informal time to think and talk about things is being lost. Yes that's right...that's really made me think.

your failings and develop yourself in a way that you want rather than following someone's lead who is telling you what you should do; and that might be adults or friends but there is a pressure to 'do the right thing'. Who knows what the right thing might turn out to be?

While we were doing our research we kept noticing things in magazines or books that were 'useful'. I wasn't sure about how you did this when we started, but studying things and noticing when people had written about the things we were talking about and I was experiencing, it made it real. I could see that these were experiences that others had had and somehow I didn't feel so alone with my fears and ideas. Even the words of songs and poems started to mean a lot more to me, and seeing this made me want to read more, even in the harder books that we used people had said things about these problems.

'For some people the day comes when they have to declare the great Yes or the great No.
It's clear at once who has the Yes ready within him; and saying it, he goes from honour to honour, strong in his conviction.
He who refuses does not repent. Asked again, he'd still say No. Yet that No—the right No— drags him down all his life.'

(Che Fece...Il Gran Rifiuto by C.P Cavafy—1990 The Collected Poems)

CHAPTER SIX

Strategies for Emancipation

The true opposite of depression is neither gaiety nor absence of pain, but vitality—the freedom to experience spontaneous feelings. [...] But this freedom cannot be achieved if its childhood roots are cut off. Our access to the true self is possible only when we no longer have to be afraid of the intense emotional world of early childhood. Once we have experienced and become familiar with this world, it is no longer strange and threatening. We no longer need to keep it hidden behind the prison walls of illusion. We know now who and what caused our pain, and it is exactly this knowledge that gives us freedom at last from the old pain.'
(Miller, 1995:71)

'As a clinical psychologist I think I would measure success in a number of ways and not necessarily to do with returning to school, it's obviously a bonus for some children and their parents but I think the measure of success for us is symptom relief and that is on the surface level and probably behind that improved well being, improved communication skills, assertiveness having a vision of future life.'

How many of these young people have no vision of future life? *Something that has come up quite a lot and made a real difference to Gemma was getting this vision*

Liminality
(a threshold - the place between trauma and recovery)

Veterinary nursing:

Ever since I was small, I have absolutely adored animals and I always said that I would be a vet and own a Lizard, a Cat and a green and white Dalmatian (don't ask!) We always had pets in the house and my Mum and Dad taught me to respect them. When you're a kid and you like animals, I suppose the most obvious job you plan to do in the future is be a vet but when I got into my teens I started to prefer the idea of Veterinary Nursing instead. This may have been due to the fact I didn't think I was clever enough to be a vet though over time I did actually like nursing better, but I can never really remember when that idea started.

When I left school at fourteen, I never thought I would be a Veterinary Nurse. It felt even more unlikely when I knew there wasn't much chance of me doing GCSEs and I thought you couldn't get any where without them. I dismissed the idea of nursing for a long time and tried to think what I could do instead. To be honest there wasn't anything else I liked better and so I tried not to think about the future too much because I didn't think I had one. I probably tried hard to stay a child so the future wouldn't matter.

After starting the Referral Centre, my teacher and the nurse there told me I was good at writing so I thought maybe I could do that if nothing else worked out. It helped to hear that I had some abilities because praise didn't happen very often in my first secondary school so it made me think maybe a future was possible.

People began again to ask me what

sorted out...and we talked about it on the way today...that after a while when you believe that it's all going wrong and you are not going to be able to do what you wanted to do with your life then it's actually easier to say to adults who say 'what do you want to do when you leave school?' 'I don't know': it's a lot easier than whittering on about something that you think now is a lost cause.

One of the conversations that we had that moved things forward after writing the story was when I said, 'OK if you had the dream scenario and none of this had happened to you, what would you have liked to do with your life?' In a sad and withdrawn voice she said, 'No-one ever asked me that before – I wanted to be a veterinary nurse but I know now that I can't.'

I said, 'Why not?' and she said, 'Well I've blown it, I've had two years off school so I'm going to have no qualifications and I won't be able to take any now.' Gemma, I said, if you were telling me that you wanted to be a brain surgeon then I might have to concede that it was significant that you had had this time off school and you weren't in the A level set, but you are not telling me that...what you want to do is perfectly possible and attainable. It is not rocket science, you can do this with NVQs and other types of qualification which we can organise for you. You will have to work harder to build up your basic skills but it's possible to do.'

Her face was transformed; she just looked at me for a long moment and then said, 'OK, so with a bit of hard

I wanted to do like they do whey you are a child and so for a time I said I was interested in writing but deep inside I kept the idea of working with animals. One day when we were talking, and trying to plan my course programme Lesleyann said, 'If all this hadn't happened to you, if you had stayed at school and been a normal school achiever, what would you have wanted to do with your life?' What a question! It so surprised me that al! that pent up longing sort of poured out of me like a tidal wave. I told Lesleyann that in the past I wanted to be a veterinary nurse and actually still would. I thought she was going to say, 'Oh well never mind...I'm sure there is something else.' But she surprised me and said, 'Well if you had said that you wanted to be a brain surgeon or even a vet, then that might have been a bit difficult, but a veterinary nurse, that's probably possible.' I was quite shocked to be told that despite everything, it could happen. A vet would have been too ambitious for someone in my position but nursing was do-able - Wow! I hadn't wrecked it; I might get back my dream. I talked and talked about it; she must have got really bored but she just listened like she always did.

I got quite excited about the idea because I had sort of lost hope on that so suddenly I decided that I had a real chance to turn this around and that was going to be my aim for the future. All of the course planning seemed to have a reason; seemed to be worthwhile, more than just to get some qualifications; this was about getting useful ones for my future. Lesleyann and I thought about what sort of skills I might need to get the sort of job I wanted, to get on to a qualifying course for vet nursing. Not GCSEs but other things that were more attached to work –vocational qualifications and some adult courses, and we put together a programme, I could see how it would work; some of the things might seem difficult at first because I had missed so much schooling, but with an aim I could make myself work harder and stick at it. The vision of being a veterinary nurse was *work I can do what I really want to do!' And that was when I managed to get her to go to the Heritage centre; this was something that had been proposed as a possibility at her recent case conference but largely ignored by her as just being a ploy to get her into being with other young people and school work.*

Together we worked out what sort of qualifications might be required, what sort of courses would be available to adults or community learners that she could be part of. I crossed my fingers that there would be a place for her on each of these. I had no qualms about her ability to do the work; all our activities to date had been about increasing her study skills, learning to type, to read for information, to plan research, to file and organise materials. The challenge would be getting her into a room with other young people and maintaining attendance..

Something else became important then—my ability to get the ball rolling to make her see that the real world of work was possible for her. What is the point of saying that something is possible if you make no effort to begin the process? Encouraging a young person to work hard when there is no obvious end-result is a betrayal of trust. Young people must be enabled to see the 'bigger picture' for their efforts and know it to be both credible and viable. I talked to a local farmer and my local vet about a voluntary placement. They both responded very positively. The vet wanted to wait until their present student had completed but could certainly offer Gemma a place the following January—I had about 3 months

there again; it was going to be worth a bit of effort.

I started the Heritage centre after choosing courses that we thought applied to animal careers as well as helping catch up on standard skills like maths and English. Not long after I started, Lesleyann helped me to find a voluntary work placement at a local veterinary practice so I could get some experience and see if I really did like the nursing side of being with animals. I started in January 2003 and I have to say I was nervous but I really wanted to see it through because it was extremely important to me. Back then I was still very shy and I had lost many social skills but the Referral Centre had done enough to prepare me and set the ball rolling.

It was hard at first and I did sometimes think I couldn't do it; there were a couple of missed sessions, which was really silly but people helped me to think it through sensibly, I sorted my head out, I gave it time and things got so much better. I learnt that I definitely wanted to be a Veterinary Nurse so there was certainly no doubt about that in the end. It was a great feeling caring for animals when they were ill or injured. I was prepared for the mess and gore and always just got on with whatever was needed. Some people just imagine that job as hugging animals every day; it's really not, there is some of that which is wonderful but there is hard stuff too. It was hard seeing an RTA (road traffic accident) cat for the first time but she was so sweet and she needed to feel safe again so that I forgot about what she looked like and I just helped to mend her. In the end she recovered, which was fantastic. They don't all get better, and I had to deal with that too, but with the support of the staff, I did and could honestly say at my college interview that I wasn't stupidly sentimental about animals and I did know about the down sides of working with them. The receptionist at the vet said to Lesleyann that 'Gemma never minds getting her hands dirty, and it happens a lot here!'

to ensure that she gained enough confidence to maintain attendance at a situation that would test her as a young person to the extreme. Being a volunteer might mean being given all the worst tasks, it might actually discourage rather than encourage her, but at least it would be a real rather than a theoretical test of her convictions. She started at the farm straight away and learned to love calves, feed lambs, stack fleeces and be with new people.

At the vet surgery, Gemma was given a lot of caring and cleaning tasks. I took her down in the mornings and collected her in the afternoons. We chose Monday as the day for this activity as it had been the worse day to motivate her to get out of bed. I dreaded weekends; it had become impossible for her to get to the Heritage Centre on a Monday so we exchanged Monday courses for dressmaking to ensure that she had a fully occupied week with a 'good start'. Now, I reasoned, doing her 'dream job' instead of dressmaking might get her through Mondays; and it worked.

On only one occasion did she refuse to go to the surgery. I arrived to collect her and she wouldn't come out of her room. I left without reasoning with her; I just couldn't understand why she would do that and I'm afraid I lost patience with her on that occasion: she knew it by the fact that I just didn't discuss it. She rang me at lunch time apologised for behaving SO stupidly and said that she had arranged to go down at lunch time herself—her Dad would take her. On reflection this had to happen,

I learnt a lot about working life at the practice and I got to know particular members of staff really well. I felt a real sense of belonging there, and that will help me when I have to start again with a job. It's always difficult at the beginning to settle in; that's not about me and my problems, it's like that for everyone, I've learned that too. I worked at the vet's for two and a half years in the end. Part of the time was in conjunction with my first year of college so I could use the vets as the work placement for the course. Having a work placement before I got to college helped me to realise that it was going to happen. I had really started on my career, the one I had always wanted.

Towards the end of my time at the Heritage centre I had to decide what I needed to do next. I still really wanted to be a Veterinary Nurse especially after having proper experience at Old Hall veterinary practice. People suggested that I could go to college in order to achieve further qualifications but I wasn't too sure because I hardly knew anything about it. I pictured college as this huge place– a bigger version of school, really, filled with loads of confident young people and me in the middle of it, not having a clue where I was supposed to go.

By chance, Lesleyann met a woman who works as a student officer at a local college that provides animal courses. To give me an idea of what colleges in general are like Lesleyann arranged an informal visit for us to look around campus with this woman. I said I would go but to be honest I thought there is no way I'm going to like this and it will be a complete waste of time. Even at that stage I always automatically came up the most negative thoughts possible for every situation I was unsure of but I was getting better at coping with it so I remained quite calm and I didn't panic.

When I got there it was a lot smaller than I had imagined and it looked quite friendly. We met up with the lady who she had to take control of her own emotions and recognise them for what they are. It never occurred again.

The staff at the vet surgery gradually increased her responsibilities and even paid her for holiday work. Before we knew it she had been there over a year and had even begun to answer the telephone and work in reception when asked. By taking on reception tasks she could use this work placement to build her 'Customer Service NVQ' portfolio and her assessor visited her at the surgery to observe her. Both work environments were linked together and Gemma could see that the world of work was about maximising the benefit of what you do. Slowly and surely she began to complete courses and gain awards. The farm work was recorded for an OCR portfolio—everything was useful.

The first award was her ECDL (European Computer Driving Licence), then Key Skills Numeracy, and Literacy. Remarkably, to gain her literacy and communication award she had to make a presentation to a group of people. She worked hard on the research for that and then just did it. No-one was more surprised than her at her presenting skills and audience control, it was such a good moment for her.

She feels now on reflection that it is quite important to remember that you can get into this thinking mode of: 'I can't do what I really want to do so therefore there is no point talking about it or thinking about it or saying to these adults anything

was very nice, just ordinary and chatty and quite young, and she showed us round the whole campus including the bar! I really liked the Animal Academy inside because it had all different species of animals in different rooms. I particularly loved the iguana called Deirdre who loves being stroked on the head and there were other animals like snakes, Senegal's and ferrets too.

I was really surprised by how much I liked it and couldn't really say anything to fault it. I was even more surprised when I found myself filling in the application form a few days later. I was going to do a foundation course, I thought that was all I would be allowed to do with no GCSEs. The lady who showed us round said that owing to my experience at the vets and on the farm, I would probably be just repeating what I already know so in the in end I chose the Animal Management National Certificate and filled everything in and posted it off. Wow! I did that.

I went for an interview about a month later and took some of my completed files from the Heritage centre. I showed the course leader my OCR farm portfolio (*I had worked on my neighbour's farm for a year to do that, up every morning at 7a.m.!*) my reflective journal notes from the vets and my numeracy portfolio. I told her about the communications level 2 and the ECDL computer course. She asked me questions like my reason for wanting to do the course and whether there were any animals that I couldn't cope with. She also asked if I would be requiring any extra support with my work. I did pause for a moment but realised I really didn't need or want help any more so I said 'No'. She said that on the basis of my work, I should be going for the National Diploma course, not just the Certificate. It was so great seeing how impressed she was with what I had done and I was so pleased that I had taken the folders and could explain them properly. Making the work look as good as I could had really been worth the effort; taking it with me was just so important. It gave *about it because I can't do it.' You then say, 'I don't know,' because if you have lost the vision what is the point of doing any sort of classes any more because it won't now be worth it, so just stay at home.*

Yes and as a clinical psychologist I think it would be very easy to rely solely on an initial assessment where the young person said, 'I don't know,' and just leave it at that. I think the children who come to the day unit get much more opportunity to explore what their options could be; certainly the children we see in the groups or in longer term therapy we hope to gradually get them to look ...*I wonder how much they bury the vision to the extent that they can't remember any more what they wanted to do...*That's an interesting question which I can't answer specifically. The 'I don't know' is a typical adolescent answer because it's a way of coping with the relentless questions of adults and getting them to leave you alone. *And I guess then that parents say, 'She doesn't know what she wants to do when she leaves school,' and this becomes the 'understanding' that is held in common.* Yes, yes, that's right, it's a dismissive strategy that gets rid of people and stops you having to think about it which is especially useful if people accept it at face value.

Are children able to de-centre? Donaldson (1978) suggests that children are egocentric; self-centred in the way that they look out at the world from their own position in it, literally or metaphorically. They fail, she says, *'to realise how the same world, seen from a different stance,*

me something to talk about and show and that made everything easier. Then she said, 'On the strength of this work and talking to you I am going to do something that I have never done before...'

I was offered an unconditional place on the course, which I was seriously shocked about but I felt so excited that I couldn't stop smiling for the rest of that week.

After the six weeks. holiday, it was time for me to start College. The day before I felt really weird but I wasn't sick with worry. It was like a calm fear mixed with happiness a sort of fizzing excitement, but the on actual morning of college I felt extremely strange. I woke up feeling scared, excited, sick and a bit shaky too. It was all a bit over whelming and the first thing I did was cry and then laugh. I told Steph who was sitting at the end of my bed that I didn't know how I felt and why I was acting like that but she understood completely. For some deranged reason she gave me two sheep ornaments for good luck on my first day and for some other deranged reason I took them! (Sheep are a big thing up here, they are everywhere and I do really like them.)

Once I got up I felt calmish but a bit sort of buzzy inside. I didn't know this at the time but every time I walked past the kitchen to get something, my Dad had to stop jumping for joy in his dressing gown behind my back! I thought my parents would be overbearing that day but they were quite cool to my face though my Mum did keep calling me 'student' for about a month instead of just Gem!

I got a ride with Lesleyann to catch my bus and I'm so glad it wasn't my Dad because I might have killed him for being too cheerful, which I really hate when I'm nervous. I felt fine when I got on the bus and think the buzzy feeling lasted all day, which was the only thing that kept me going.

I went to reception when I arrived with the sheep clanking around in my bag would appear—or what meaning the same words, heard and interpreted by a different brain with a different store of previous knowledge and experience, would carry.' We may be quite comfortable about this notion with regard to very young children but we may have assumed too much maturity in this sense, of older children.. Certainly in my 'conversational' work with Gemma when I was asking her to consider how different people might view the same situation, how a reporter or observer might view a scene; how a victim or the perpetrator of an incident might see it; she only gradually began to be able to see that there could be other points of view. Then through discussion she identified that these other witnesses' opinions are coloured by beliefs, values, expectation, levels of maturity and experience. *'OK, so I might have been reading something into that look or gesture that wasn't really there and then being me I just made it worse and worse...and they didn't realise how it made me feel, well, not as deeply as I was feeling it because it wouldn't have affected them in that way...mmm...making more sense now.'*

They can't put it into words...one of the breakthroughs I had with Gemma was during our work on using metaphor and analogy. I gave her some examples of stories written by adults about incidents in professional practice through turning them into metaphor, and I suggested that she might like to try and do this herself. This was hard reading for her, but it was nothing like schoolwork. She came up with an amazing story with all sorts of

and there were quite a few people squashed in there. I was by the door and this girl came past and said, 'Excuse me.' I had been told to report at reception then go to the sports hall for a 'welcome to college' thing but I didn't know where it was so I thought maybe I should ask that girl, I grabbed my courage with both hands and I'm so glad I did because I found out she was on the same course as me which took a lot of pressure off. We went to look for the hall together then stayed together for the rest of the day. We met other people on the course and had an introduction with the course leader. That was basically it and I quite enjoyed myself during some parts. It was weird being in my own without support and surrounded by all these people but it wasn't horrible at all. It was just like a blur really and when I got home I remember I was physically shaking and feeling knackered but for the first time in ages I actually felt proud of myself.

Friends and confidence

I went to college for two years and I got my Diploma which meant that I produced work that was of merit and distinction quality, me with my non-traditional qualifications! The first year was quite tough because I needed to make friends and it had been so long I had forgotten how to do it. People said that I was really quiet in the first year but I still managed to make a small group of friends. Unfortunately my two closest friends at that time, left at the beginning of the second year! I felt really crappy about that at first but it gave me a chance to get closer to another girl I sort of knew. In the first year we didn't really get on that well, partly due to my shyness and also because we never really clicked as I preferred talking to the other two more. In the second year we were forced together after they left and anyway I was a lot more confident so we became quite close and confided in each other. We also mixed with other girls on the course and I became close with a couple of them in particular.

key elements in it that she had never talked about before. I let her explain her metaphors as we talked through the story. While she was writing it she would interrupt our work, particularly if we were doing some dressmaking for relaxation, by asking things like 'what could I use to try and express…?'

I think she began to explore a bit what these thoughts and feelings were, plus because it was a story it gave her a way of saying things 'in disguise', surfacing difficult ideas. There was an incredible transformation in how she rationalised situations once we got this story out of the way.

As a referral centre when you produce a profile about a young person I am assuming that most of the things I have listed are part of it? I'm not so sure that **learning style** would figure hugely because we are not educational, **thinking styles** might well be there and I would really be interested in the thinking styles of the family. Because some families are more reflective than others and some more psychologically minded than others so that's important.

Confidence and self-esteem are important. **Group interaction and dynamics**, and again we would be looking at family interaction and dynamics and asking questions about peer relations but probably not having much opportunity to see them in action so we would be relying on other people's reports like teachers. Having said that, when children come into the day unit we would see them interacting but that is in very small numbers

Qualifications and assertiveness

I surprised myself when I started college because I really wasn't sure what was going to happen and how much it would change things. From the moment I found out I had a place, I had a good gut feeling about it and most of the time I think my intuition leads me to the right things or pulls me back from stuff that I'm likely to regret. I learnt during college to listen to my intuition so now I know the difference between not doing something because you're scared and not doing something because you know it's not right for you. I knew college was right for me and so I told myself if I did ever feel afraid I should just shove it aside and keep thinking about my dream job at the end of it. I used what I learnt with Lesleyann during those difficult years to overcome any future problems before they had the chance to happen, I got much better at reading situations and people. The knowledge of an unconditional place at college gave a boost in self belief before I started and the fact I had achieved other things that I wasn't sure about also made me feel good about going. The fact that no one in college knew about my past and would only find out if I told them was also really good; it put me in control of who could have my 'hidden' information.

When you are being helped it can feel really difficult because you are aware that the people who are supporting you know about your problems, so they are sort of treading on eggshells with you; the places you go like the pupil referral unit and the Heritage Centre sort of exist for people like you so you can't be anything but 'needy'. I got sick of needy and wanted to be who I am from now. College needed to be a fresh start for me, a clean page especially with the other students, and it was. Lesleyann did do a special letter to go with the application form so that the college would understand why I was entering with nontraditional qualifications and what she as an academic thought of my ability; but she also said that entry and I know very well that children can come in here and appear to be supremely confident and then go down the road to the secondary school and fall apart.

Body language and behavioural signals - yes we would be taking notice of and asking questions about that.

Personal space needs – that's interesting... *that's come out of what we have been talking about in terms of invasion of personal space and whether classrooms are much more invasive of your personal space...*that's very interesting, really interesting, especially with the transition from small rural primary to huge secondary schools...*it came up from my point of view because I have done a lot of work with autistic children and personal space is a big issue – it's the thing you look for first because it might help you the most once you understand that individual's needs. But I think that it is much more widespread in terms of how people react when their personal space is invaded. I felt that it was something that maybe would come into this school phobia problem for some children, certainly peer to peer.*

Some peer interactions are invasive and that is why it is interpreted by the victim as bullying... it is what you are saying about some adults might not see this type of bullying... but to some children having a child here (hand held 15 cms from face) or even 60cms away, if you perceive that to be your 'personal space', then that is being bullied even if that child is smiling at you: it is the fact of proximity. Exactly and

was as far as that information was to go and once I was there, I stood or fell by my own ability although she did offer to support my academic work if I chose that. If I chose it! What a long way I had come. She let me read the letter first and I agreed to it. I know that it helped me to get an interview, but after that I also know that I did the rest myself.

Standing out

From the age of fourteen until about seventeen, I got into the habit of wearing unusual clothes. I made a point of not wearing anything that was too fashionable or clothes that I would imagine other girls my age wearing. The most obvious thing to do when you are a person such as I was is to try and blend in or be invisible but to be honest at the time, deep down, I was sick of being invisible. I was actually just desperate for someone to understand me, the hidden me. I couldn't do that by making friends because I couldn't talk to anyone or even look them in the eye for any length of time. So I tried to demonstrate 'me' silently through my appearance.

I suppose I was trying to show people who I was by wearing particular clothes that would show off my style. Some outfits were quite bold or brightly coloured and I was really into decorative ethnic objects and patterns too. After I started college I really began to accept myself and felt more confident in my personality to the point I stopped using my appearance to compensate as much as I had been doing. I didn't go back to how I dressed before my problems started but I just settled for wearing what I like and what suits me regardless of whether it is in fashion or not. The only problem with the bold style was that I hated wearing anything in fashion in case I blended in and even if I liked something that fitted with that style but that was in fashion I would always think twice before putting it on. When I was seventeen, I matured a great deal and decided it was pretty thick to not wear something for that reason so

I think being in the changing room with teenagers changing for PE in front of a baying crowd or not, just being exposed in that way to others is the same issue.

Communication initiation and repair – *the ability to repair communication is something that I think is underestimated in terms of a social skill.* Yes I agree. *When someone goes off on another tack how easy is it for a communication partner to pull back the conversation to what they want it to be about?* What comes to mind here is something to do with the way in which people in the family communicate as well, because often we would see families where the young person doesn't get a chance to say anything because someone is talking for them...so we would be looking at style there and opportunity for communication.

I think we are always thinking about this next one—**gender issues** and things like if the young person is a girl should they see a woman therapist? - for example in the regional clinic where I work there is a nurse who did see Gemma initially. The reason for that is that you never quite know what is going on and we do see children who have been abused and who disclose abuse and who are not going to school for that sort of reason, less commonly but it does happen. Who you communicate with, that's important, we don't automatically assume that the young person is going to be able to talk with the person who takes the referral.

Gemma is a reasonably bright girl; if she had not had the difficulties

I binned that idea and I just wore what I really wanted to wear, fashion or not. I'm a sort of mixture now of fashionable and a special sort of personal style. I have started mixing some of the more bold stuff with other things but just to suit myself, and the occasion.

I did change over time in the Heritage Centre but I didn't want to show it then because I felt people expected me to act the same as I had been when I first went there. I'm glad in a way because I saved my new changes for college in order to make a new start. My friends did find out about my past by accident when I was asked about my non-existent GCSEs but I explained and they understood. That's what friends do. Although I was quiet at the start and it felt difficult I just decided to learn the social thing as I went along and in the second year my friends told me I had changed a lot. In the end I began to feel really comfortable talking within a group of people I knew. I relaxed and decided to loosen my grip on control. After years of trying to protect myself by not doing things I realised it was all negative (refusing to let others get close, refusing to do new stuff). I chose to let go a bit because it's only then that you do actually have a bit of control. You need to find a balance between letting things happen and making things happen. In my case I used to stop things happening and even made things stop through my stubbornness!

As time moved on I really felt so much better about myself. I had a social life again and I started going on nights out in Carlisle and having a laugh, I started to have numbers on my mobile phone, people to call and people who called me. One of my first friends was the one who taught me to worry less; she was very carefree and cheerful about everything. I realised it didn't really matter if I got things wrong or if I came across as a bit thick, which I sometimes do! Just as long as you're a decent person then nothing else matters too much because there is such a thing as being too clever as well at school which reduced her attendance levels to something barely reasonable then she would clearly have been able to achieve at least the minimum of GCSEs to pursue whatever career that she wanted to do. She is artistic and enjoys creative activities; in this way she has leanings towards the sort of activities that I enjoy when not pursuing my academic career. We got on well. In the early days of working with Gemma I was keen to assess and build upon her basic 'study skills. She was not attending school so what I did with her had to feel like something meaningful. I am a qualified teacher and planning a credible individual education plan for a particular pupil was easily achieved. At first I believed that I would just teach her how to undertake research, help her with the academic side of that in terms of selecting and reading appropriate theory and encourage her to explore her difficulties through guided reflection.

She was able to handle that type of work for long periods of time; we visited libraries, she learned how to look for key words and suitable texts, to scan read and look for passages that had resonance for her. I did not though, want this work to become dull for her so once we had our timetable of work sorted out I introduced some more creative elements to the days that we were together. We made a working miniature theatre for her sister's birthday and she wanted to try to make moving curtains so had to learn how to use the sewing machine. This lead inevitably to me talking to her about the possibility of making her own clothes. She had

as being a twat! The girl, who I became friends with later, taught me to be tougher again, as she is quite blunt but in a nice way so now I'm learning to say no, rather than trying to please everyone all the time.

I learnt a lot about animals during the course and there was never a day I didn't attend out of fear, because I knew how important it was and I knew the pattern too well. One odd day can very easily lead to a fortnight.

One of my extra subjects with Lesleyann was dressmaking, I was learning how to design and make patterns and clothes and a lot of ideas came from Indian and Bohemian type designs, some of which I looked up on the internet. I was also keeping a 'style file', a sort of scrapbook of all the pictures I found that I liked: clothes, furnishings, makeup, animals, anything really that appealed to me. I was developing an idea of the sort of person I wanted to be, the sort of house that I might like, a sort of insight into who I was. I kept to the same style for quite a while and it did help me a lot. I was trying to regain my identity because I felt like I was a nobody and completely insignificant so I needed this new understanding of myself and my style to make me feel as though I was worth a bit more than that. My personality at the time made me practically non-existent and I hated that but back then I couldn't do anything about it so I used something else, my appearance, to try and show that I wasn't as I seemed. I made some wild and some beautiful clothes, some of which I still wear.

Changing my room:

When something happens to you that turns things upside down and affects everything in your life, sometimes your whole existence freezes. One moment I was thirteen and although my life wasn't perfect because the bullying had started I still had a life.

to learn how to make patterns from her ideas using existing clothes as models and select appropriate materials to use.

The dressmaking 'study skills' utilised her creativity, gave her some practical skills and made use of my own expertise. All adults have something they can share with a young person while they are talking to them. It makes it less 'therapeutic' and creates a far less confrontational communication position because you are almost never face to face in these circumstances and this is very liberating for the speaker. They can chat, ask questions, probe answers and look for reflective solutions whilst apparently 'doing something else.'

Our chats matured as Gemma matured. We developed a comfortable way of being together and having shared so much we became good friends. However much Gemma achieved in terms of her qualifications, work experience and college place, there was still pressure on her to 'have friends' like other young people. The first thing that one of the school teachers said to me when I told him of her course successes was, 'But does she have any friends yet?

No-one can produce friends for you; this is most certainly something that you have to do yourself when you feel confident enough. During my normal work I happened to have a meeting at the college, Gemma passed by my room chatting away with a group of young women. She rushed up to me to say, 'Hi, lovely to see you but I must dash; I'm just off with my friends.'

Life stopped when I stopped attending school and so did everything in it. I was unable to grow up properly because I had no friends with whom to share experiences and learn with. It is impossible to develop as a person when you are alone so part of my personality wasn't maturing like it would have if I had been with people my own age. I fell behind my peers socially and emotionally as well as academically. I did mature in some ways but other things stopped for a while.

Basically I was a thirteen-year-old, then everything in my world went black and there was a gap and then suddenly I was a seventeen-year-old starting adulthood. That was quite an adjustment. Even my personal environment didn't seem to change properly. My bedroom stayed quite similar for a long time, and it was a young girl's bedroom really. I kept all the old clutter because it made me feel comforted and reminded me of when things were better. When I started college, I grew up really quickly. I had to do that in order to catch up with everyone else. I noticed then that everything started moving again and I felt so different. I put the clutter in the loft, things which were sentimentally attached to the past but suddenly seemed stupid now.

I kept important things but threw out things that would remind me of my 'darker days' like a decorated ladder I made with Lesleyann when I was sixteen and which I used when I had achieved a day at the Heritage Centre. (One day = one rung higher.) I didn't need this stuff any more. I also noticed that for the first time in ages I had birthday and Christmas cards from friends displayed in my window. My life started again and so everything else around me moved with it. I realised that just like the song. I had:

'Reached for the hero inside myself, looked at the secrets I hide, reached for the hero inside myself, ' and then I got 'the key to my life.'

BIBLIOGRAPHY AND REFERENCES

Bandura, A. (1986) *Social Foundations of Thoughts and Action* (Englewood Cliffs, NJ: Prentice Hall)

Bentley,T. (1998) *Learning Beyond the Classroom* ((Demos) London: Routledge/Falmer)

Cavafy, C.P. (1990) 'Che Fece II Gran Rifiuto' from *The Collected Poems* translated by Edmund Keeley and Phillip Sherrard (London: Hogarth Press)

Claxton, G. (1990) *Teaching to Learn* (London: Cassell)

Craft, A. (1996) *Continuing Professional Development* (Buckingham: OU Press)

DfES (2003) 14-19 *Opportunity & Excellence* (HMSO)

Donaldson, M. (1978) *Children's Minds* (London: Fontana)

Erikson, E.H. (1963) *Childhood and Society* (New York: Norton)

Evans,N. (2002) *The Smoke Jumper* (London: Corgi)

Follett, M. (1924) *Creative Experience* (New York: Longmans Green)

Fullen, M. (1999) *Change Forces:The Sequel* (London: Falmer)

Furedi, F. (2004) *Therapy Culture* (London: Routledge)

Goleman, D. (1996) *Emotional Intelligence*(London: Bloomsbury Publishing)

Goleman, D. (1998) *Working with Emotional Intelligence* (London: Bloomsbury Publishing)

Miller, A. (1995 *Edition*) *The Drama of Being a Child* (London: Virago)

North Patterson, R. (2000) *Dark Lady* (London: Arrow)

Orbach, S. (2001) *What's Really Going on Here?* (London: Virago)

Polanyi, M. (1977) *Meaning* (London: University of Chicago Press)

Rodriques *et al* (1959) *'The outcome of school phobia.'* American Journal of Psychiatry No.116 pp 540-544

Salkovskis (Prof.) (2006) *Walking to Freedom - (Mail on Sunday* magazine)

Spencer, J. (1996) *Homesong* (Hammersmith: Harper Collins)

Tyerman Williams, J (1997) *Pooh and the Philosophers* (London: Methuen)

Valles, E. & Oddy, M. (1984) *The Influence of a return to school on the long-term adjustment of school refusers'*, Journal of Adolescence No7 pp35-44

Ward, I. (2001) *Phobia* (Cambridge: Icon Books)

AUTHORS' BIOGRAPHIES

Gemma Osborne

Gemma Osborne was born in Basildon, Essex in 1987 and has a younger sister, Steph. Growing up in Wickford she attended the local infants and juniors school.

Gemma experienced her first taste of bullying on attending secondary school before moving to Cumbria two years later. Although hoping to leave the bullying behind Gemma experienced more bullying and stopped attending school at fourteen. Aged fifteen, Gemma began 'alternative education' and, gradually, her fears were replaced with achievements.

Having a love of animals, Gemma gained a diploma in Animal Management and works voluntarily for a veterinary practice with the aim of becoming a qualified Veterinary Nurse.

Lesleyann Morgan

Born in Singapore in 1949, Lesleyann Morgan qualified as a primary teacher in 1970 with a Certificate of Education. She has extensive educational experience in both statutory and special education as a teacher, manager and specialist advisor.

Lesleyann began working with a university school of education in 1996 as a guest lecturer and then as a head of department teaching research skills to mature students who were teachers doing a part-time higher degree.

Gaining an MA in education 1998 and PhD in Educational Research in 2001, Lesleyann retired in 2000 but continued as a freelance consultant on local and national Higher and Further Eductation and Local Education Authority Research.